"North

Volume One

Civil War Stories From Mount Airy and Surry County

Also by Thomas D. Perry

Beyond Mayberry: A Memoir of Andy Griffith and Mount Airy Mount Airy North Carolina

Ascent To Glory: The Genealogy of J. E. B. Stuart

The Free State of Patrick: Patrick County Virginia In The Civil War

Images of America: Patrick County Virginia

Images of America: Henry County Virginia

Then and Now: Patrick County Virginia

Notes From The Free State Of Patrick

God's Will Be Done: The Christian Life of J. E. B. Stuart

Patrick County Oral History Project: A Guide

Upward Toil: The Lester Family of Henry County Virginia

Mount Airy, North Carolina

Martinsville, Virginia

Henry County Heritage Book Volume One

J. E. B. Stuart Birthplace: A History

Fieldale, Virginia

"If Thee Must Fight, Fight Well." William J. Palmer and the Fight for Martinsville, April 8, 1865

The Graham Mansion: A History

Ghosts of the Graham Mansion

"The Dear Old Hills of Patrick" J. E. B. Stuart and Patrick County

Visit www.freestateofpatrick.com for more information

"North Carolina Has Done Nobly"

Volume One

Civil War Stories From Mount Airy and Surry County

By

Thomas D. Perry

Copyright 2013 Thomas David Perry

ISBN-13: 978-1478235163
ISBN-10: 1478235160

Laurel Hill Publishing LLC
P. O. Box 11
4443 Ararat Highway
Ararat, VA 24053
www.freestateofpatrick.com
276-692-5300
freestateofpatrick@yahoo.com

Cover and title page are Confederate Veterans Reunion in Mount Airy, North Carolina. (Courtesy of the Surry County Historical Society.)

For Christian's Uncles

John and Galen Cail

Major General J. E. B. Stuart was born just outside Mount Airy, North Carolina, in present day Ararat, Patrick County, Virginia, and frequently wrote about and visited the town.

"If anyone speaks to you of subjugation, tell them it shows a total ignorance of what constitutes our armies. Long after the inhabitants crouch to the conqueror our armies will tread with the triumph of victories freemen over the dead bodies of the vainglorious foes. North Carolina has done nobly in this army. Never allow her troops to be abused in your presence."
J. E. B. Stuart

This book is the first in a proposed series about North Carolina and the Civil War. The second title will cover J. E. B. Stuart's cavalry regiments from North Carolina.

Contents

Foreword John Cail's Book	11
Chapter One War	19
Chapter Two J. E. B. Stuart's North Carolina Connections	25
Chapter Three A War Between the States Photo Album	67
Chapter Four Jonathan Hanby Carter	103
Chapter Five The Siamese Twins in the Civil War	109
Chapter Six William Norman	125
Chapter Seven Who Shot John Reynolds?	143
Chapter Eight Tar Heel	147
Chapter Nine Stoneman's 1865 Raid	155
Afterword Andy's Civil War	203
Bibliography	209
Index	211

William W. Ward

Foreword

John Cail's Book

Near the end of 2012, John Cail let me borrow a book from his vast Civil War book collection. The best Civil War library in northwestern North Carolina might be a few blocks behind Central Methodist Church just off North Main Street in Mount Airy, North Carolina. The book was *"For the Sake of My Country" The Diary of Colonel W. W. Ward 9th Tennessee Cavalry, Morgan's Brigade C.S.A.*

For many years, John Cail and I ran the Surry County Civil War Round Table that met mainly at the Mount Airy Public Library on Rockford Street. An offshoot group started the James Ewell Brown Camp #1598 Camp of the Sons of Confederate Veterans that I served as First Lieutenant Commander in the 1990s and again in the late 2000s, but due to low numbers and having to do most of the programs, John and I gave up on the idea of a Civil War Round Table.

This culminated in an off and on interest in the War Between the States between us that included many tours of battlefields from Gettysburg, Pennsylvania, to Chickamauga in northern Georgia, just south of my father's birthplace, Chattanooga, Tennessee. These trips included Mike Hayes, George Speight, and John's brother, Galen Cail.

On one memorable trip John, Galen, and I found ourselves at the Brotherton Cabin at Chickamauga. I found the spot my father's collateral ancestor's regiment, the 17th Tennessee Infantry. My father, Erie Perry's great-great uncle, John D. Lynch, of Sherwood, Franklin County, Tennessee served in Company I of this regiment. Lynch lost a leg on the second day of the battle on September 20, 1863, probably on Snodgrass Hill that included a breakthrough at the spot where I found myself standing that was the beginning of an assault on Snodgrass Hill that nearly destroyed the Union Army.

Confederate General Bushrod Johnson commanding our ancestors wrote of the attack. "The scene now presented was unspeakably grand. The resolute and impetuous charge, the rush of our heavy columns sweeping out from the shadow and gloom of the forest into the open fields flooded with sunlight, the glitter of arms, the onward dash of artillery and mounted men, the retreat of the foe, the shouts of the hosts of our army, the dust, the smoke, the noise of fire-arms—of whistling balls and grape-shot and of bursting shell—made up a battle scene of unsurpassed grandeur."

George Thomas, "The Rock of Chickamauga," himself a native Virginian stayed loyal to the Union and did great service at Chickamauga. John, Galen, and I discovered that our family members did great service for their country, the Confederate States of America, that day. As I gazed at the plaque for the 17th Tennessee, I looked up the road to find John standing at the next plaque several yards away for the 54th Virginia Infantry. His family served in a company from Floyd County, Virginia. To make the cliché that it is a small world seem irrelevant; we discovered that our families fought side by side at this battle. John and I continued this connection with our study of the conflict that nearly tore our nation apart.

The book John loaned me might seem to have nothing to do with Mount Airy or Surry County, North Carolina in the Civil War, but that would be wrong. William Walker Ward was born on October 5, 1825, near Carthage, Smith County, Tennessee. The six foot two inch Ward had hazel eyes and light brown hair. He became a lawyer practicing for a decade before the outbreak of war in 1861.

Like many Southern men, Ward opposed secession, but when war came, he enlisted in Company B of the 7th Tennessee Infantry on May 20, 1861. He served in western Virginia including time with Thomas J. "Stonewall" Jackson in the 1862 Romney Campaign. Ward received a discharge on May 19, 1862, due to an ankle injury.

If you cannot walk, then ride. Ward joined the 15th Tennessee Battalion of cavalry as a sergeant and then became a captain and began to form a company of his own men. Placed under the command of Kentuckian John Hunt Morgan, it became "one of the very best in Morgan's command" commanded by Colonel James D. Bennett.

The regiment saw its first combat under the command of Joe Wheeler at Goodlettsville, Tennessee, where Union cavalry routed it. Ward took it upon himself to improve the performance of his men. Although he had no formal military training, he was known as a disciplinarian. Basil Duke described him as "intelligent, zealous, and firm." Ward "constantly drilled and instructed his men."

As part of "Bennett's Cavalry" in Morgan's command, the regiment was part of the attack on Hartsville on December 7, 1862, that killed or wounded 200 Yankees and took 1,800 prisoners. "Ward's Ducks," as his men were called for their ability to ford streams, were part of Morgan's famous Christmas Raid.

Along the way, Ward married Elizabeth Hughes Rucks, sister of Lt. Howell Rucks, Jr. of Company D. The couple spent their very cold wedding night under a wagon on December 23, 1862, the same day Ward received promotion to Colonel of the regiment after Bennett died.

Morgan's raid covered over 500 miles in Kentucky and Tennessee. Ward's regiment was reorganized as the 9th Tennessee Cavalry. They participated in Morgan's raid over the Ohio River in the summer of 1863. Union forces captured Morgan and Ward on July 19, 1863, near Buffington Island in the Ohio River. He was first jailed first in Cincinnati, Ohio, then imprisoned on Johnson's Island in Lake Erie, and then transferred to the State Prison in Columbus, Ohio on August 1, where Ward was "strip searched, shaved, bathed, and placed under close confinement."

On March 28, 1864, Union officials transferred Ward to

Fort Delaware on Pea Patch Island in the Delaware River, where he started the diary that became the book that John Cail let me borrow. Ward left Delaware on June 28 for Charleston, South Carolina, where he was exchanged on August 4. He began a trip from Charleston to Abingdon, Virginia via stagecoach, railroad and two horse "gig" that led him to Surry County, North Carolina. If the reader turns to page 75 of the book, they will discover the following passage.

"Thursday, August 11th, 1864

Take breakfast at Mr. Chissums at 6 A. M. and leave Salem on a two horse hack at 6 ½ for Mount Airy. Mr. Vest one of the proprietors of this line and one of the drivers is quite clever. Webber, Myself, Patterson and two passengers (Soldiers) we had yesterday make up our crowd today. We pass over a very poor country. Citizens ignorant and very poor. At the first stand we get some fine peaches. At the second stand lives old Mr. Gordon who is the father in law of my old friend Dr. Davis' sister. I did not see her. A few miles after we left the stand I met Dr. Davis and a Mr. Gordon. The old Dr. was delighted to meet me, offered to treat me on good brandy of which he said he had one hundred gallons and was selling it out at ($100.00) one hundred dollars per gallon. The old fellow was truly glad to see me. He has been absent from home about one year. His Mother has recently died. We arrive in Mount Airy at 8 o'clock P. M. Pass old Mr. Armfields just before getting to the little town. He is a brother or near relative of General Armfield of Tennessee. The old land lord pays $10,000 tax, is rich and niggardly. Near on to one bushel of chinches inhabited each bed in the room we were put in to sleep. Bill $10 for supper and lodging. This day we take dinner at Mr. Daltons, quite a nice place. We get a good dinner for $5. This is in sight of the Pilot Knob, which is a magnificent sight to behold. We travel in a few miles of it rather around its base near a half day."

Some explanation of those mentioned. Mr. Vest was Lewis M. Vest, who subcontracted and was co-owner of the stagecoach line running from Salem (it was not Winston-Salem yet) to Mount Airy. Mr. Gordon was Francis H. Gordon, a relative through marriage to the Wards. Dr. Davis was Dr. L. H. Davis, a native of Surry County, who practiced medicine in central Tennessee before the Civil War. Mr. Armfield was Isaac Armfield, a Surry County farmer, whose farm was valued at $5,000 in 1860. Mr. Dalton was

David N. Dalton of Stokes County, who served as postmaster at Little Yadkin.

Morgan escaped with several of his men from the Columbus Prison. Ward rejoined his command and learned of the death of Morgan at Greeneville, Tennessee.

Ward became commander of the 1st Kentucky Battalion under Basil Duke. Ward received a battle wound in the leg at Bull's Gap. His diary ends on April 6, 1865. He died on April 10, 1871, and is buried at his wife's family cemetery near Rome, Tennessee.

Over the years, John Cail and I continued to get together, have dinner and talk the war. I came to admire John and his brother Galen not just for their interest in our common history, but for the way they as Christian men took an interest in their nephew Christian, a teenager at this writing and a great musician. The Cail brothers are a great example of men taking their responsibilities as role models seriously and for that, this book is dedicated to them with great respect.

Chapter One

War

The biggest grossing movie of all time is *Gone With The Wind.* Scarlett O'Hara spoke at the beginning of the film of her disgust over talk about the "War, War, War." The war fought between 1861 and 1865 nearly broke this nation apart. As I write this book, the nation is commemorating the 150th anniversary of the war. Twenty-five years ago, it was a much bigger deal with the release of Ken Burn's PBS documentary, *The Civil War.* The interest in the war is suffering from a lack of interest in history in the schools and the focus on social history away from the military history. Many believe that the obsession with "political correctness" has hurt the interest in the war as no one wants to be labeled a "racist" by studying or showing interest in those who fought to preserve slavery.

My professor at Virginia Tech, Dr. James I. Robertson, Jr. always told us that no one would ever understand what the United States is today without a knowledge of the war. Whether it is States' Rights or Civil Rights all these subjects related to the war. Whether you call it the Civil War, War Between the States, War of

Northern Aggression, or the War for Southern Independence, there is no doubt that, the war was one of the most important events in our nation's long history as a Democratic Republic.

The question of the cause of the Civil War is still a controversial topic. Academics will claim slavery was the only cause while "Confederate-Americans" talk of states' rights.

The fact is men and women fight civil wars over power, political power. That power might include the right to keep slaves or the power to protect goods with tariffs, but it is always about power.

It is now estimated that over 700,000 men lost their lives between 1861 and 1865 fighting this war. North Carolina for years bragged of being "First at Bethel, Farthest at Gettysburg and Chickamauga and Last at Appomattox." For years, North Carolina was thought to have supplied and lost the most men, but recent research proves "The Old North State" usurped in this claim by Virginia.

North Carolina was last to secede from the United States of America on May 20, 1861. The people of the state and Surry County were not fire breathing secessionists.

Surry County had 10,380 people in the Census of 1860 with nearly 9,000 whites, 1,200 slaves and 134 free people of color. There were 1,600 households and 193 of these owned slaves. Mount Airy had 300 people.

When President Abraham Lincoln maneuvered the South Carolinians into firing on Fort Sumter in April 1861, he then called for 75,000 volunteers to put down the "rebellion." Lincoln and the United States government referred to the conflict as the "War of the Rebellion" believing the Southerners had no right to secede and refused to recognize the Confederate States of America as a viable entity.

Governor Ellis of North Carolina responded to Lincoln's call for troops. "I regard the levy of troops made by the administration for the purpose of subjugating the states of the South as in violation of the Constitution and a gross usurpation of power I can be no party to the violation of laws of this country and to this war upon the liberties of a free people. You can get no troops from North Carolina."

On August 14, 1942, Joseph H. Fulton, who lived at his family home called "Linger Longer" along present day Riverside

Drive in Mount Airy told of the beginning of the war in Mount Airy. He stated three or four companies mustered in on Lebanon Hill, where they camped and drilled for several weeks. The day before the men "marched away to battle," they had a barbeque, a very North Carolina thing to do considering that from the time of William Byrd's survey of the dividing line between North Carolina and Virginia until today eating pork has been a staple of the diet. The men went down the Old Westfield Road towards Danville, Virginia, where "they got guns."

One of those men was Bazilla Yancy Graves was born to Soloman and Mary Moore Graves in 1835. He was the Captain of Company C of the 21st North Carolina Infantry starting on the day North Carolina left the Union on May 20, 1861. Promoted to Major on May 25, 1862, Graves received a wound in the leg later that summer. He received promotion to Lieutenant Colonel on August 28, 1862. On September 1, he received a wound in the right arm and shoulder at Ox Hill, Virginia. Reported absent wounded the following year, Graves did not return to service. He became the first mayor of Mount Airy for two months from May to July 1885. He rests today on Lot 20 in Oakdale Cemetery.

The following companies came from Surry County.

Company H, 21st North Carolina Infantry

Company C, 21st North Carolina Infantry

Company A, 28th North Carolina Infantry

Company B, 2nd Battalion North Carolina Infantry

Company B, 2nd North Carolina Infantry

Company I, 37th Battalion Virginia Cavalry

Company I, 18th North Carolina Infantry

Company E, 53rd North Carolina Infantry

Company I, 45th North Carolina Infantry

Reflecting a different time, William Carter, another Mayor of Mount Airy wrote in his book *Footprints in the Hollows*. "This war, a war fought to preserve those freedoms which the states had written into the Constitution in 1787. The record of Surry's delegates who signed this document made it clear that they believed in the right of the states to withdraw from the Union if and when it was deemed best of their people."

Future North Carolina Governor Zebulon Vance wrote, "If war must come, I prefer to be with my own people. If we had to shed blood, I prefer to shed northern blood rather than southern blood. If we had to slay, I had rather slay strangers than my own kindred and neighbors; it is better whether right or wrong that communities and states should go together and face the horrors of war in a body sharing common fate, rather than endure the calamities of internecine strife. The argument having ceased and the sword being drawn, all classes in the South unite as by magic."

Over 100,000 men from North Carolina went off to fight the war. Over 1,000 of them came from Surry County. In 1992, Hester Bartlett Jackson released *Surry County Soldiers in the Civil War,* which contains a roster and more information about these men from Surry County who fought in War Between the States.

Chapter Two

J. E. B. Stuart's North Carolina Connections

On August 5, 1854, newly graduated from the United States Military Academy at West Point, New York, Brevet Second Lieutenant James Ewell Brown "Jeb" Stuart found himself at a crossroads in life and on his travels that year. Soon the United States Army ordered him west to Texas to join the Regiment of Mounted Rifles. Stuart took the opportunity to visit family and friends that summer across piedmont Virginia and North Carolina. On this night, he was camping on a local mountain the natives called Jomeokee, meaning "great guide" or "pilot." Watchers of the Andy Griffith Show might call it Mount Pilot, the home of the "Fun Girls," but the rest of the world calls it Pilot Mountain. Peter Jefferson and Joshua Fry listed this mountain on their map as Mount Ararat, but today only the river that flows by it now uses that name.

During the night thunder, lightning and a storm woke young James Stuart and inspired him to write a poem dedicated to his younger sister, Victoria, titled *The Dream of Youth.* It began with,

"Twas night, and o'er the sable garb that hung,

Around the Pilot's base, a ray was flung…"

Thirty lines later, Stuart ended his poem with these lines,

"Twas all a dream, such are the dreams of youth,

Alas, how many hearts have felt this truth!

Such dreams have often tantalized my soul

And bourne me oft to my ambition's goal."

Stuart reached his "ambition's goal" achieving fame and glory as a soldier for seven years under the flag of the United States of America and then three years under the flag of the Confederate States of America making him the most historical person and most famous non-entertainer from the region that includes Mount Airy and Surry County, North Carolina.

This chapter tells his story and his many connections to Mount Airy and Surry County. It also tells of his connections to the "Old North State," the home of Stuart's Tarheels, the men of five regiments of cavalry, who served under Stuart from North Carolina in the War Between the States. North Carolina was a place he thought of positively in spite of his ties to the

Commonwealth of Virginia.

Upon arriving at the United States Military Academy at West Point, New York, in 1850 J. E. B. Stuart wrote, "I might have rambled the dear old hills of Patrick amid all the pleasures of a mountain home for a life time." Stuart also rambled the hills of piedmont of "The Old North State" during his time at home in 1852. Two years later, he returned after graduating thirteenth in a class of forty-six. He slipped from as high as seventh in his class. The family tradition holds that he gave up studies to have a good time, so he could be a cavalryman instead of an engineer, where the top of the class received assignment. Stuart by age twenty had traveled to New York and back to his Virginia home, but during this time (1852 and 1854), he visited many places in North Carolina.

Surry County was not the only place in North Carolina he visited in 1852 when on leave from the United States Military Academy and after he graduated two years later. He went to the Hairston Family home, Sauratown along the Dan River along the Rockingham and Stokes County lines. Many noted his likeness to his sister Columbia as she was married to Peter Hairston and lived at Cooleemee Plantation in Davie County.

Stuart wrote, "I intended telling you a few of my adventures, such as being taken for a horse drover in North Carolina and repeatedly bantered for a horse swap, asked if I belonged to Mr.'s _____ Circus, my being recognized at Saura town by my likeness to Lummie(Columbia L. Stuart Hairston), on my presenting myself at the pay office in Washington how the clerk persisted that I was dead and finally after I perseveringly protested that I was alive concluded that it was some other 'Stuart,' but we will I hope laugh over these some other time."

Stuart assisted with the construction of Cooleemee and may have obtained architectural drawings for his brother in law Peter Hairston. In an April 13, 1852, letter from Stuart to Peter W. Hairston, the former commented that he was looking for plans for the house. The design of the home came from W. H. Raulett's The *Architect* published in 1849 and was in the library at the United States Military Academy at West Point, New York.

Stuart wrote, "I take pleasure in informing you that 'all's right' at Cooleemee Hill. Your house is progressing rapidly the brick had risen more than half way up the second story window and door frames." The house built by Conrad and William of Raleigh, North Carolina, included Lieutenant Stuart as a construction worker. Mr. William, the architect even built a wagon for Columbia's son, Sammy. Stuart wrote of his nephew, "Sammy came out wonderfully before I left. He seemed to rival me as a master of ceremonies and excelled me in gallantry for he gathered a beautiful bouquet of rosebuds and presented them to Miss Fanny Shepperd." Five years later in 1859, Stuart's West Point classmate William Dorsey Pender married Miss Fanny Shepperd in present day Winston-Salem.

Stuart visited Congressman Augustine Shepperd, who lived at the present day corners of Vargrave and Waughtown streets in Winston-Salem. Augustine Henry Shepperd represented North Carolina in the U. S. House of Representatives. Born in Rockford, Surry County, on February 24, 1792, Shepperd studied law, was admitted to the bar, and commenced practice. He served as a member of the North Carolina House from 1822 until 1826. He went to Congress first as a Jacksonian in the Twentieth through Twenty-second Congresses, reelected as an Anti-Jacksonian to the Twenty-third and Twenty-fourth Congresses, then was reelected as a Whig to the Twenty-fifth Congress. He served as Chairman of the Committee on Expenditures in the Department of the Navy, the Committee on Expenditures in the Department of War, the Committee on Expenditures in the Department of State chairman, and the Committee on Public Expenditures. He lost reelection in 1838 to the Twenty-sixth Congress. He returned to Congress as a Whig in the Twenty-seventh Congress. Elected as a Whig to the Thirtieth and Thirty-first Congresses, he declined to be a candidate for reelection in 1850. He returned to the practice of law and died at "Good Spring," Salem (now Winston-Salem), Forsyth County, on July 11, 1864, with interment in Salem Cemetery, just two months after J. E. B. Stuart passed away in Richmond.

Stuart kept his sister Columbia's spirits up that summer noting, "I kept her laughing as long as I stayed by making myself ridiculous in various ways." Was this something he continued in his military career showing an ability to put on a mask to achieve his goal? Did this translate into Stuart's cavalier dress with the red cape and plumed hat? Certainly, it shows that he was more than capable of considering the concept of bringing attention to himself to keep the morale of his men and his sister high during distressing times.

A slave at Cooleemee, John Goolsby, claimed to know why the South lost the war saying, "Marse Jeb was too fond of the ladies and Marse Jubal was too fond of the bottle." J. E. B. Stuart and Jubal Early were not only both Confederate Generals involved in the controversy surrounding the Battle of Gettysburg, but also were both cousins to the Hairstons.

Stuart's wrote of his miserly ways during his travels. "It almost grieves me when I find myself unable to do justice to a meal for which I have to pay full price, for it has always been my consolation that I always got the worth of my money in the eating line and precious little did a hotel keeper ever make off me."

He borrowed $150.00 from his brother-in-law, Peter W. Hairston, in July 1854 to "outfit himself for frontier duty." He visited another sister Victoria at Salem Female Academy.

Another stop for Stuart was the home of Nicholas Lanier Williams, "God's Hill," on Panther Creek in Forsyth County built in 1766 by Colonel Joseph Williams. Stuart noted, "I left Cooleemee Hill Tuesday evening for Mr. W's wishing to see my friends there once more before leaving the Country." Williams known for his hospitality that Stuart enjoyed and his "Old Nick Whiskey" that Stuart no doubt did not partake of as he was a teetotaler, was a member of the council of state and trustee at the University of North Carolina at Chapel Hill.

In his August 3, 1854, letter, Stuart wrote of Dr. Swan and Dr A. M. Nesbitt of Water Street, two doors down from J. F. Chamber's store in Salisbury, North Carolina. They were taking care of J. A. Lillington of North Main Street on Mocksville. Stuart heard Reverend James G. Jacocks of St. Luke's Episcopal Church in Salisbury preach in Mocksville near Cooleemee in Davie County, North Carolina.

In 1854 during his travels through the Tar Heel State, Stuart dined in Mocksville and was amused by hypochondriac Episcopal minister who when told of a cholera epidemic got sicker as the story was relayed to him. He left for Patrick County that day and spent the night on Pilot Mountain where the thunderstorm already mentioned woke him on August 4, 1854.

The Stuart connections to Mount Airy began years earlier when Elizabeth Letcher Pannill married Archibald Stuart and came to Laurel Hill in the mid 1820s. Their property bumped up against the Virginia-North Carolina border just five miles up present day Riverside Drive from Mount Airy. Elizabeth's eighth child, a boy was born on February 6, 1833. They named him James Ewell Brown Stuart after the brother in law of Archibald Stuart, James Ewell Brown, who was a Judge in nearby Wythe County,.

James spent the first twelve years of his life at Laurel Hill before going to Wythe and Pulaski Counties to continue his education around 1845. Three years later, he studied at the Methodist Emory and Henry College in Southwest Virginia for two years before receiving an appointment to the United States Military Academy at West Point, New York, in 1850. He graduated four years later and became a brevet second lieutenant in the United States Army. During that summer of 1854, he camped on the side of Pilot Mountain in Surry County and wrote about his dreams and his ambition's goals.

The following year (1855) as his mother made her way to Mount Airy to attend church. According to local tradition Elizabeth Stuart stopped at "Linger Longer," the home of Joseph H. Fulton, a few miles closer to town and changed into her best bonnet from the everyday bonnet she wore at home.

Educator and local historian Ruth Minick called me one day in the early 1990s to tell me she had something to donate to the effort to preserve Stuart's Birthplace. The story she told me went like this. In 1859, John Henry Jackson, a major in the local home guard attended an auction at Laurel Hill. Mrs. Stuart moved to Danville after she sold some of the household items. Jackson purchased a bell at the sale in 1859. Ruth called to offer it to the Stuart Birthplace for future display. Jackson was the maternal grandfather of Mrs. C. D. (Ruth Smith) Lucas.

Mrs. Lucas, who was also a relative of Mrs. R. J. Reynolds (Katherine Smith of Mount Airy), wished to donate the item. Today it is one of the few items thought to be from Laurel Hill. Interestingly enough another is a blanket chest once in the possession of Attorney Martin F. Clark, Sr. of Stuart, Virginia.

Another story often told the author, also from Ruth Smith Lucas, daughter of Zack Smith, was that Elizabeth Stuart often stopped by their home to "refresh herself" on the way into town. In the aftermath of the Civil War, many people in Mount Airy began to associate stories with the Stuart family.

A year earlier the redheaded son of Elizabeth, James Ewell

Brown Stuart, rode his horse along the same route to Mount Airy possibly with his mother to attend church, for shopping excursions with his sister Victoria in what became "Granite City." He wanted to pick up the family mail. James E. B. Stuart was hoping for a letter from a young woman, Elizabeth Perkins Hairston.

The Stuart's route into Mount Airy, North Carolina, from their farm, Laurel Hill, in Ararat, Virginia, took them near the world's largest open-faced granite quarry, which along with tobacco and furniture factories would bring the railroad to the town after the war that took James E. B. Stuart's life. The Stuarts left the area almost one hundred years before Andy Griffith would make Mount Airy famous as the fictitious North Carolina town of Mayberry on television.

In the summer of 1854, Brevet Second Lieutenant J. E. B. Stuart rode down what is today Main Street in Mount Airy, North Carolina. The "Granite City" young Stuart rode into was a place getting ready to explode with tobacco and textile concerns.

Stuart rode into town on the Old Springs Road and up Lebanon Hill where he passed the Methodist Church first built two years before his birth where many congregations met including the

Episcopalians, forerunners of Trinity Episcopal today. The church bulletin claims that two of Stuart's sisters received confirmation in 1852. Built on land deeded from the Roberts Family, the two-room log structure covered by clapboards had granite pillars and steps with a lean-to attached to the building for Negro worshippers.

The strongest local tradition involving the Stuarts in Mount Airy is that the family attended church services there. The Methodist Church on the north side of Lebanon Hill began services in 1831. Elizabeth L. P. Stuart was a "High Church" Episcopalian and the evidence points to her attending the congregation of Trinity Episcopal Church who meet today in Mount Airy's oldest building. Evidence suggests that the Episcopal congregation met on Lebanon Hill in the Lebanon Methodist Church.

The first entry in the parish register of Trinity Episcopal Church reads, "The first account on any service of the Episcopal Church in Mount Airy was during the Episcopate of Bishop Ives, the year not remembered, when in old Lebanon Methodist Church (north of town) he confirmed the sisters of General Stewart of Patrick County Virginia." Tradition holds the year was 1852, but there are doubts about this. The trend in Mount Airy to associate people, buildings and even churches with the Stuart family after the rise in fame of J. E. B. Stuart in the War Between the States, is commonplace in Surry and Patrick Counties.

A program from the 1980s for Trinity Episcopal Church in Mount Airy, North Carolina, contains the following. "Episcopal services were inaugurated in Mount Airy in 1852 when Bishop Stillman Ives confirmed the sisters of General J. E. B. Stuart. Construction of Trinity Church began in the spring of 1896, and the first service occurred in July. The building is an identical copy of a chapel in Oxford, England, and the ivy on the outside walls was rooted from cutting brought directly from Oxford."

Levi Stillman Ives was born in Connecticut on September 16, 1797. Ordained a priest in the Protestant Episcopal Church in 1823, he received election as Bishop of North Carolina in 1831. He held the post until 1852. He worked for religious training of slaves. Ives started the Society of the Holy Cross, a monastic order of the Anglican Communion in 1842 situated in "Valle Crucis," the Valley of the Cross, the Saint Andrews Cross in western North Carolina. In 1848, he began publishing "doctrines" objectionable to the diocese. On December 22, 1852, Ives renounced the

Episcopal Church and made formal submission to the Roman Catholic Pope. He died in New York City on October 13, 1867.

So, did the "Right Reverend" Levi Stillman Ives cross paths with the Stuart Family in Mount Airy, North Carolina as the bulletin for Trinity Episcopal Church claims? Robert Merritt graciously shared his research material with the author on this subject. He and his wife, Cama, are two of the guiding forces in the Surry County Historical Society. Robert points out that Ted Malone of the Diocesan House says, "Bishop Ives confirmed the sisters of J. E. B. Stuart before one of them married Peter Hairston." This would be Columbia Lafayette Stuart Hairston (1830-1857), who married Peter Hairston in 1849, three years before the traditional confirmation date. It is doubtful that Columbia returned to Mount Airy from Davie County to receive confirmation.

However, when dealing with oral traditions, is it possible that Ives confirmed another younger sister of General Stuart in 1852. Victoria born in 1838 is the obvious choice, but Virginia, who was born in 1836 and died in 1842, did not live long enough. Merritt points out that 1852 is possible as the journals of Bishop

Ives from 1852 are missing and he did travel to the northwest counties of North Carolina especially "Wilkesborough" and the "Valley of the Yadkin" south of Mount Airy. He does mention Ives visiting Surry County twice at Rockford along the Yadkin River on the southern boundary of the county, but there is not one instance mentioned of Ives visiting Mount Airy. The record about the confirmation written in 1896, forty-four years after the event, leads this author to believe that possibly one sister of General Stuart received confirmation, but it is doubtful that the event occurred. It may be another example of Mount Airy latching onto the fame of a famous Confederate officer in the post war period of the "Lost Cause."

There is much evidence that the Stuarts did attend church in the town. Five years later on September 18, 1857, Victoria Stuart wrote Bettie Hairston about subjects dealing with Mount Airy. She wrote, "We got home very safely the day after we left Beaver Creek. I have not been anywhere since except to preaching." She wrote of her "Brother James" telling Bettie of his wounding at the hands of the Cheyenne at a battle along the Solomon River in Kansas. The following year she noted in another letter dated April

17, 1858, "Excuse my nice letter paper, as it is the best Mount Airy affords." Victoria made sure to tell Bettie about her former beau, the now married Lieutenant J. E. B. Stuart of the First U. S. Cavalry casually mentioning, "Brother Jim has gone on the Utah expedition."

As the Stuarts made their way into town, the rode past the Robert Galloway home. Galloway donated the land across the street from his home for what is today First Baptist Church. He built an Opera House that opened on January 6, 1891, and still stands today on Main Street in Mount Airy occupied by Brannock and Hiatt Furniture.

When Stuart approached the main business district in 1854, where many financial institutions now stand, he saw a business and residential area down to Renfrew's (Renfro's) Hill, the site of the post office today. Then it was the home of Doctor Joseph Hollingsworth, the Stuart's family physician.

When Archibald Stuart first arrived at Laurel Hill in 1825, the Stuarts knew the town as Mount Airy, although it was sixty years before the town incorporated using the name. There are at least ten communities named Mount Airy all over the country including Mount Airy, Maryland, along with towns in Georgia, Louisiana, Missouri, New Jersey, Ohio, Pennsylvania, New York, and in Pittsylvania County, Virginia, just north of Perkins Ferry on the Dan River is Mount Airy, Virginia. It is from the connection with this family named Perkins that the North Carolina town got its name.

Mount Airy sits near the confluence of the Ararat River with Lovills and Stewarts creeks on the stage line between Wytheville, Virginia, and Salem, North Carolina. History records inhabitation at Mount Airy as early as 1747. Granite from the quarry nearby began operations as early as 1775. The first business district was where Hamburg Street crosses the Ararat River near the present day Mount Airy Middle School. In the 1820s, the business district moved to the present day area along Main Street.

Arriving on Main Street in Mount Airy, J. E. B. Stuart saw the Blue Ridge Hotel run at that time by Colonel Harrison Waugh, but started by Stuart's Perkins relatives. Thomas Perkins wrote the following passage in his will dated April 17, 1816, listed on page 138 of Surry Will Book Number 3, "To my son Constantine Whitehead Perkins I give my land including the seat where I now live called and known by the name of Mount Airy." The source for most of this material is *The Descendants of Nicholas Perkins* by William Hall.

Nicholas Perkins came to Virginia in 1641. By 1650, he had 170 acres in the Bermuda Hundred area on the James River near Richmond and died six years later in Charles City County. His family would spread out across our country into present day Kentucky, Tennessee and Surry County, North Carolina. The descendants of two of his sons Philemon (born circa 1680 in Henrico County, Virginia and died in 1769 in Goochland County, Virginia) and Constantine (1682-1770) brought their families to the region.

Philemon (born circa 1720 in Henrico County, Virginia, and died in 1793 in Caswell County, North Carolina) married Obedience Cox and had Abram, who had Philemon. The latter Philemon died in 1795 in Pittsylvania County, Virginia. He married Mary Whitehead and they had Thomas Perkins. Son Thomas received 68 acres from his father and the 1811 Pittsylvania County, Virginia, records list him paying taxes on it. Thomas married twice, first to Faithey (Faithy) Peebles. Their children were Constantine, Polly who married a Buckley and then a Walker, Elizabeth, Nancy who married John Martin, Amy who married a Robertson and then a Massey and Peter Peoples Perkins. In 1798, Thomas sold his land in Rockingham County, North Carolina, on the south bank of the Haw River and moved to Surry County. A genealogical chart showing these relationships follows.

The other son of the first Nicholas Perkins, Constantine, married Anne Pollard. Their son Nicholas married Bethenia Harding. The Perkins family lived on the Dan River in Pittsylvania County, Virginia. One of their homes, Berry Hill, still stands on the banks of the Dan River built by Nicholas and Bethenia's son, Peter. Peter's sister Elizabeth Perkins married William Letcher in 1778. They moved to Henry County (Patrick County today) settling along the Ararat River, a mere six miles from Mount Airy, North Carolina. They were J. E. B. Stuart's great-grandparents.

Another interesting side story to Thomas Perkins is the executors of his will: Michajah Oglesby, Jonathon Unthank, and Jesse Franklin. Jesse Franklin (1760-1823) married Maacah Perkins (1766-1834). She was the daughter of Hardin Perkins (1730-1795) and Sarah Price. Hardin was the younger brother of

Nicholas Perkins, the father of Elizabeth Perkins Letcher Hairston. These two prominent families connected via marriage. Franklin was Governor of North Carolina along with serving in both the United States House of Representatives and Senate.

Thomas Perkins, a distant cousin of the Stuarts, owned Mount Airy Plantation, which gave the town its name. His son Constantine left another mark on the small North Carolina town of Mount Airy in the form of the lodging establishment he began. The Blue Ridge Inn or Blue Ridge Hotel would be the first of four establishments on the corner of Main and Oak Streets over the next one hundred and fifty years. In 1819, there is evidence that the town was to become Perkinsville. Constantine sold off lots around 1823 among to one Gallahue Moore and around that year built Mr. Perkins's Hotel. Tradition holds this building contained the first post office for the town. Perkins's brother in law Dabney Walker ran a stagecoach line that stopped at the hotel. Fire destroyed the wooden structure.

Perkins sold the hotel to Thomas B. Wright, who was postmaster in 1835. Wright built the second of four hotels on the site and the one brick structure in one of the earliest known buildings in town between 1835 and 1840. It went into receivership and was sold in 1849 to Allen Denny who ran the hotel until he died in 1878. By the 1890s, J. K. Reynolds owned the facility. In 1891, Reynolds had designed a new hotel- a grand three-story building with more than 100 rooms and electricity. Called the Blue Ridge Inn, it was short lived. It burned down in the "great fire" on January 1, 1892, which destroyed an entire city block. A group of businessmen lead by Rufus Roberts rebuilt the fourth structure to its grandest level again of brick until demolished in 1965.

Local tradition abounds about young James E. B. Stuart coming into Mount Airy. During the preservation efforts begun in 1990, many older women of the town told this author stories of their ancestors dancing "The German" with Stuart at the Blue Ridge Hotel, but sadly there is no documentation. In a 1936 article in the Mount Airy Times, John D. Thompson told Hugh Merritt that, "J. E. B. Stuart would go to the balls and ladies would fall down in a swoon." In addition, the story of Stuart planting boxwoods around town originates from Thompson.

With all the stories lacking documentation, it reminded this author of William Letcher, J. E. B. Stuart's great-grandfather, who died during the American Revolution and received a promotion in every book about J. E. B. Stuart after the latter became famous. Letcher was a Captain in the first biography of his great-grandson, but was a Colonel by the middle of the twentieth century. In reality, he was a Corporal in the Henry County Militia.

J. E. B. Stuart rode up to the front of Robert Gilmer's store, where the post office had recently moved from the Blue Ridge Hotel. The hotel was not always the location of the post office. Many men served as Post Master of Mount Airy. The earliest evidence starts with Jonathan Unthank, the original owner of the Mount Airy Plantation, which was located in present day Bannertown. The 1822 post office was at the home possibly due to the political connection from Unthank's marriage to Governor Jesse Franklin's daughter.

Allen Denny owned the Blue Ridge Hotel in 1848 and served as postmaster. The hotel built by Thomas Wright in 1835, who also served as postmaster. Robert Gilmer served in 1850 when Colonel Harrison Waugh owned the hotel.

Young James E. B. Stuart visited the post office often

looking for a letter from his cousin Bettie Hairston of Beaver Creek plantation in Henry County. A family story says Stuart proposed to her, but she turned him down because she did not think he would amount to much. She literally kept the money in the family by marrying cousin J. T. W "Watt" Hairston, who served on General Stuart's staff during the Civil War.

In January 1, 1855, "Jeb" wrote from Texas to his cousin Bettie Hairston at Beaver Creek Plantation in Henry County, Virginia, "I attended the Post Office at Mount Airy, North Carolina regularly the short time I remained at home but was often disappointed by finding no letter from Beaver Creek." Four days later Stuart again mentioned the town writing again to Bettie, "Your long expected and anxiously looked for letter I found here on my arrival yesterday. I attended the Post Office at Mount Airy, North Carolina regularly the short time I remained at home but was as often disappointed by finding no letter." There is more to the story. During his one term as a member of the United States House of Representatives (1837-1839), Archibald Stuart accomplished one thing. He established a "Star" mail route between Mount Airy and Ararat, Virginia, which existed into this author's lifetime.

During the end of 1854-1855, Bettie Hairston was not the only young woman who noticed James Ewell Brown Stuart. Robert Gilmer's daughter, Elizabeth Anne "Lizzie" Gilmer (1835-1898), wrote often in her diary about the Stuarts now in the collection of the Mount Airy Museum of Regional History. She wrote of a visit with the Stuarts on March 31, 1855, "Took a very pleasant ride out to Mrs. Stuart's with Brother John and Miss McQueen. No doubt our visit would have been more pleasant if one absent member of the family could have been there." Was the missing member the twenty-one year old recently graduated Lieutenant Stuart? We will never know for sure, but it is hard to imagine that a young man recently graduated from West Point walking around Mount Airy in uniform would not have attracted her attention.

"Lizzie" Gilmer visited Laurel Hill on February 24-25, 1855. Earlier in the month she wrote, "Miss McQueen and I spoke of going to Mrs. Stuart's today, but have postponed it until next Saturday." She wrote on February 24, "Miss McQueen and myself went to Mrs. Stuarts, enjoyed the ride very much notwithstanding Old Gray; was my steed." She wrote the next day, "We were received with so much kindness. Life has some green spots. I never enjoyed a visit more. Vic (Victoria Stuart) is almost my ideal of beauty – so good and so noble too. The friendship of such a one is one of the strongest ties that bind me to earth." Miss McQueen was a music teacher from Nova Scotia. Both "Lizzie" and "Vic" attended the Salem, North Carolina, Female Academy from January 1852 until June 1853, as did Bettie Hairston. Gilmer wrote on April 1, 1855, "Returned home from a visit that was more than pleasant. Vic is one my dearest favorites. She is a beautiful girl, amiable, intelligent and unaffected."

Robert S. Gilmer purchased a home in 1845 from Jacob Brower. He owned the land including the granite quarry. In 1858, "the vine was planted" when the Gilmer Family formed the First Presbyterian Church in Mount Airy. Services were held originally at the Gilmer's home, later at the Methodist Church on Lebanon Hill and in 1873 at the present site starting in a frame building now replaced by a granite structure.

On January 13, 1855, Elizabeth "Lizzie" Gilmer wrote about church services on Lebanon Hill. Gilmer a Presbyterian like many attended the multi-denominational services at the Methodist Meeting House on Lebanon Hill. She wrote, "Went to Lebanon and was caught in a refreshing shower...After the doors were closed for the night, the arrival of Mrs. Stuart and family was announced; and it seems many, many faces made their appearance. How rare do we meet with one whose mind belongs to that high idea with which she may so justly be classed."

Around 1855 Elizabeth Gilmer opened the first school for girls in Mount Airy and spent most of the next forty years teaching there except for a short time in Statesville. She never married and her obituary said the following, "She sacrificed a great part of her life in caring for three aged persons, and had hoped that God would spare her life a little longer in order that she might care for and be a comfort to her father during his remaining pilgrimage on earth." There is no mention of Elizabeth Gilmer in J. E. B. Stuart's writings, but she no doubt followed his career with interest and mourned his early death and maybe "Lizzie" thought of what might have been with "Jeb."

From the post office south, there was a business block with storefronts for the Gilmers, Samuel D. Moore, Murphy and S. T. Allred, a branch of the Greensboro store of Scott and McAdoo along with W. R. Bray's Tailor Shop. As early as 1846 when Jacob

Brower's cotton and woolen mill opened in the town, textiles were part of the local economy. By 1853, tobacco processors were established.

Although no record of the encounter is known to exist, Stuart could have met some other famous nearby residents, the Chang and Eng Bunker better known as the "Siamese Twins," who resided south of town on the banks of Stewart's Creek. Eleven years later, Union cavalry under George Stoneman raided through the area commenting on the famous entertainers as the famous "Chinese Twins."

In 1859, Stuart returned east from his service in the U. S. Army. He sold the patent for an invention of "Stuart's Lightning Horse Hitcher" to the War Department. Stuart went with Robert E. Lee in October 1859 to Harper's Ferry to help put down "John Brown's Raid."

Stuart returned to North Carolina for the last time in 1859 accompanying President James Buchanan to the University of North Carolina at Chapel Hill for commencement exercises. Buchanan set out for Chapel Hill on May 30, 1859 with Messieurs Thompson and Magrow by boat from Baltimore bound for Norfolk and Raleigh. Described as "gay and frisky as a young buck," he returned to Washington City by the Tuesday before June 10.

One of his cabinet members noted, "The old gentleman was perfectly delighted with his trip." After delivering the graduation speech Buchanan greeted admirers shaking hands and kissing the girls. However, there was a serious note in Buchanan's speech, for the shadow of secession and the issue of slavery hung over the nation at the time. "Let the Union separate," he said prophetically, "and it would be the most fatal day for the liberties of the human race that ever dawned upon any land."

While James E. B. Stuart's career in the United States Army blossomed in Kansas, his mother and remaining siblings continued to live at Laurel Hill just outside Mount Airy, North Carolina, in Patrick County, Virginia.

At Cooleemee, Columbia Lafayette Stuart Hairston died during her brother's service in the U. S. Army and her two surviving children followed leaving Peter W. Hairston free to marry again and start a new family that continues to this today to live on the banks of the Yadkin River in Davie County.

In November 1855, Stuart married Flora Cooke, the

daughter of U. S. Army officer, Philip St. George Cooke. The couple had four children, but only two survived to have children of their own. Stuart rose in rank to Captain in the First U. S. Cavalry stationed at Fort Leavenworth and then Fort Riley in Kansas Territory. He rode the Santa Fe Trail, fought Cheyenne, and helped to control "Bleeding Kansas" including encountering John Brown.

James E. B. Stuart's brother, John Dabney, a surgeon in the 54th Virginia infantry, said of the coming War Between the States, "Where there is a prospect of war you will find more southern men rushing to the field of battle than you will northern men."

In May 1861, J. E. B. Stuart resigned his captaincy from the United States Army's First Cavalry and offered his sword to Virginia. Stuart commanded the 1st Virginia Cavalry at First Manassas. He received promotion to Brigadier General.

The 1st North Carolina cavalry first joined Stuart's cavalry brigade in October 1861 with officers such as Robert Ransom, Rufus Barringer, Laurence Baker and James B. Gordon of Wilkesboro.

The 2nd North Carolina Cavalry joined with General Stuart's command in November 1862, went on his famous

Dumfries raid, and chased after that legend of North Carolina historical markers, George Stoneman, during the Chancellorsville campaign.

Stuart became famous in 1862 commanding Robert E. Lee's cavalry in the Army of Northern Virginia. His troopers rode around George McClellan's Army of the Potomac three times in that year earning him a promotion to Major General after the first in the summer of 1862.

The 4th North Carolina Cavalry arrived for grand review on June 5, 1863, just before Brandy Station, but were under Beverly Robertson and with Lee, not Stuart, during the ride to Gettysburg.

The 5th North Carolina Cavalry arrived for the grand review of June 8, 1863, serving like the fourth North Carolina under the command of Beverly Robertson. Stuart had little respect for Robertson, who followed Lee's column during the early part of Gettysburg campaign and was not with Stuart.

At Brandy Station the Tar Heel troopers were part of Wade Hampton's Brigade playing an important role in the largest cavalry battle ever fought in the Western Hemisphere. Stuart's controversial role at Gettysburg occurred next with his late arrival at that battle.

During the fall/winter 1863-64, Stuart followed North Carolina Governor Zebulon Vance during the latter's visit to the Army of Northern Virginia. The 3rd North Carolina Cavalry was only with Stuart from April 1864 until his death in May.

Stuart lost his life on May 12, 1864, just north of Richmond, Virginia, when one of George Custer's Michigan troopers shot him in the abdomen at Yellow Tavern. He is buried in Richmond's Hollywood Cemetery.

While Virginia has much reason to be proud of Stuart, he would not have singled out just his troopers from the Old Dominion. In one of the last letters, he wrote his wife, Flora, in that romantic prose of his day. He had this to say, "If anyone speaks to you of subjugation, tell them it shows a total ignorance of what constitutes our armies. Long after the inhabitants crouch to the conqueror our armies will tread with the triumph of victories freemen over the dead bodies of the vainglorious foes. North Carolina has done nobly in this army. Never allow her troops to be abused in your presence."

At least one North Carolinian noted this fact because every year on February 6th Congressman Charles M. Stedman of North Carolina would rise in Congress. Stedman was the last Civil War veteran in the U. S. Congress. He obtained unanimous consent to speak for five minutes on Confederate General James Ewell Brown Stuart.

Another North Carolinian and admirer of J. E. B. Stuart summed up the image and reputation of Stuart when Thomas Wolfe wrote in November 1930, from London, England, to Alfred S. Dashiell. "You know that I am no Pollyanna now, or that I think God's in his heaven. I don't, and I agree with Ecclesiastes that the saddest day of a man's life is the day of his birth—but after that, I think the next saddest day is the day of his death. I have had some bad times recently, but I think I shall always love life and hate death, and I believe that is an article of faith. The futility people hate life, and love death, and yet they will not die; and I loathe them for it. Observe carefully: you will find that the man who kills himself is almost always the man who loves life well. The futility people do not kill themselves; they wear rubbers and are afraid of colds. The wastelander does not waste himself; it is the lover of life who wastes himself, who loves life so dearly that he will not hoard it, whose belief in life is so great that he will not save his own. I mean Christ and Coleridge and Socrates and Dostoievsky and Jeb Stuart..."

On July 9, 1859, Elizabeth Stuart sold the Laurel Hill Farm to two men from Mount Airy, North Carolina. Robert R. Galloway and Dr. Joseph Hollingsworth bought the 1500 acre Laurel Hill Farm from Elizabeth Letcher Pannill Stuart on July 9, 1859, for $12,000. Galloway received the part of the Laurel Hill Farm originally given to William Letcher Pannill from his mother Bethenia Letcher Pannill. Hollingsworth received the part given to Elizabeth Letcher Pannill Stuart that included the house site currently owned by the J. E. B. Stuart Birthplace. From 1859 until 1879, the Hollingsworth and Galloway families owned the Stuart land. Virtually no improvements to the property occurred per the Patrick County Tax Books during the time Galloway and Hollingsworth owned the property. In fact, the value of the buildings on the Laurel Hill farm went down $100 in value. The two Mount Airy men most likely rented the property out to tenant farmers and with the later owners, Laurel Hill continued as a working farm.

Robert Richard Galloway (1830-1901), the son of Charles and Sarah Michaux Galloway, came from Rockingham County, North Carolina, to Mount Airy in 1855. Before the Civil War, he married Mary Virginia Caldwell. The Caldwell land north of town included the land where Oakdale Cemetery is located. He served as a musician during the Civil War and returned to Surry County. Mary died in 1869 and five years later "Bob Dick" Galloway married Lucie A. Blackwell. He outlived both wives and produced twelve children. The Galloway home sits on 739 North Main Street in Mount Airy.

Galloway ran a tanyard and store in the town. He built the 600 seat Opera House in the town at the site of the Brannock and Hiatt building on Main Street and owned a stake in the Blue Ridge Inn, the hotel begun by the Perkins Family. Known for his philanthropy, Galloway donated the land across from his home that became the First Baptist Church. R. R. Galloway is buried in Oakdale Cemetery. He left his interest in the Stuart property to his son, Frank Galloway.

The other man to purchase the Laurel Hill Farm was Dr. Joseph Hollingsworth, one of eleven children born to James and

Elizabeth Golding Hollingsworth. Besides Joseph, two other brothers Edwin and William Hollingsworth studied medicine at the Jefferson Medical College of Philadelphia. Born ten miles southeast of Mount Airy near Tom's Creek on February 27, 1820, Joseph studied in Germanton, North Carolina, and under Dr. Beverly Jones before heading to Philadelphia, where he studied (1845-1847).

Dr. Joseph Hollingsworth (1820-1887) was the first in a long line of physicians. Hollingsworth served as an Assistant Surgeon in the Eleventh North Carolina Infantry, Surgeon in the Seventy-Third North Carolina Infantry Regiment and as a Major serving as a surgeon at the brigade level. He married Mary Letitia Banner, daughter of John E. and Virginia Moore Banner, in 1847 and had nine children. They lived near the site of Mount Airy's post office on Renfro Hill and later on South Main Street.

The tradition is that he was Elizabeth Letcher Pannill Stuart's physician and that after she left the area he traveled to take care of her in Danville and possibly Saltville, Virginia. No doubt, this relationship led Hollingsworth and Galloway to purchase Laurel Hill in 1859. Dr. Hollingsworth, described as "a finer type of the hard working, high minded and conscientious physician the annals of North Carolina medicine does not afford," is buried in the Old Settler's Cemetery of the first Mount Airy Methodist Church.

Hollingsworth was the doctor to the Siamese Twins, Eng and Chang Bunker, who lived near Mount Airy. When Eng and Chang Bunker died in January 1874, Dr. Hollingsworth over saw the autopsy of the Bunkers in Philadelphia. He believed that separating them during their lives meant certain death for them both and the autopsy proved him correct. The Mutter Museum in Philadelphia where the autopsy occurred has a plaster cast of the twins.

In 1905, the Galloway family sold 277 acres of the Laurel Hill Farm for $2,000 to J. O. Hatcher, who raised horses on the land were the famous cavalryman was born and raised. The following year Thomas Brown purchased the same property for $2,085 adjacent to the lands of the Mitchell, Jarrell, Pedigo and Galloway families. Brown bought land from the Taylors as well.

Another story connecting Laurel Hill and Hunter's Chapel Church involves the Taylor Family. Samuel H. Taylor (1820-1893) purchased seven hundred acres of the "Stuart Place" for $4,000 in 1879. Taylor served as Clerk of Superior Court for eight years in Stokes County and Sheriff of Surry County, North Carolina, from 1874 until 1881. Many believe Andy Griffith used his name for the character Andy Taylor on the Andy Griffith television show. Taylor died in 1893 and after his death, his heirs tied up the property in litigation. No change in the value of buildings occurred and the tenant farming of the Galloway-Hollingsworth years continued. This information is pertinent to the 75 acres owned by the J. E. B. Stuart Birthplace, but many families over the years owned the 1500 acres that once belonged to the Stuart family.

Other stories relating to the Stuarts in Mount Airy abound in the oral tradition. Local historian and educator Ruth Minick documented many of them. One story relates to Mrs. Stuart's "green thumb" and the boxwoods at Laurel Hill. Dr. Hollingsworth planted boxwoods from Laurel Hill and many homes in Mount Airy still have them growing in the yards.

Interestingly, Oakdale Cemetery comes from the land of Robert Galloway purchased in 1921 from the administrator of his estate, Samuel H. Taylor. In 1929, Oakdale Cemetery transplanted a boxwood from the front yard of Mrs. Susan E. Hollingsworth, the wife of Dr. William Hollingsworth, brother of Dr. Joseph Hollingsworth. This boxwood reportedly came from Laurel Hill. Mrs. Hollingsworth requested the "Box Tree" be moved to the cemetery "to assure its permanence in a public place." The plant was twelve feet high and ten feet in diameter and placed in the eastern side of the cemetery

Today, in Mount Airy's Oakdale Cemetery stands a lone holly tree giving shade to the graves of two great women who shared a love of our region's history. Many knew Miss Ruth Minick for her columns in the Mount Airy newspapers or her career as an educator. Ruth worked with this author on many projects over the years such as placing the marker for Stoneman's Raid at the Mount Airy Library. She shared her accumulated knowledge of regional history. She never let the boundary line between North Carolina and Virginia stand between her and the writing of the history on Stuart's Birthplace. She was a mentor to many of us saying, "History is like going down a river, but you never get to the end of it, because you are up in all the tributaries checking out all the coves."

During the preservation of Laurel Hill in the early 1990s, many people remembered this shared history with Surry County and Mount Airy, North Carolina. Ruth Minick wrote that our region had "a man who accomplished more of national importance, was more nationally prominent and just as famous" as Andy Griffith or the Siamese Twins. The Mount Airy News published an editorial echoing similar sentiments, "While many might consider the proposed preservation of Stuart's birthplace as an out of state project, the site is so close to Mount Airy that it would enhance tourism efforts under way in Surry County. As a matter of fact, historians say the flamboyant general spent much time in Mount Airy."

In a nearby plot in Oakdale Cemetery the last owners of the Laurel Hill Farm, Icy Bowman Brown, her husband G. E. "Shug" Brown and their two children rest. To say Icy loved history would be an understatement. Her enthusiasm for Stuart's Birthplace and preserving the site and the history surrounding it, is legendary to those of us who knew her. When this author was a boy, Icy stimulated my interest in Laurel Hill through her scrapbooks and her willingness to tell me all she knew.

Some warm summer evening when the wind blows through that holly tree, we can imagine they are discussing the history that lies on both sides of the boundary between Virginia and North Carolina. Two great ladies are together now with their families and I hope heaven gets a big dose of our history every day.

Author Tom Perry at Stuart's Birthplace, the site he worked to save at the Virginia Historical Highway Marker that first started his interest in history and J. E. B. Stuart, as a young man.

Relationships Between The Hairston, Perkins and Marr Families

Nicholas Perkins

Constantine Perkins	**Philemon Perkins (see below)**
Nicholas Perkins (1718-1762)	Abram
|- Peter married Agnes Wilson	
|-Susannah married John Marr	Philemon
|-Constantine m. Agatha Marr	
|-Elizabeth m. William Letcher	Thomas Perkins (owned Mount Airy)
|-Bethenia Letcher	
married David Pannill	Constantine Perkins
|-Elizabeth Letcher Pannill	(built Blue Ridge Inn)
married Archibald Stuart	
|-J. E. B. Stuart	

The Fulton Home "Linger Longer" was a frequent stop for the Stuarts on their way back and forth to Mount Airy.

Chapter Three

A War Between The States Photo Album

Above is a reunion of Confederate soldiers in Mount Airy between 1867 and 1919 as that is when the Jesse Moore house in the background stood. (Courtesy of the Surry County Historical Society.) Below, is the "Confederate Parade" along Renfro Street in 1914. The Leonard Jewelry Building is in the background. (Courtesy of the Surry County Historical Society.)

Daughters of Confederacy Parade
Main St., Mount Airy

The United States of America has fought many wars and continues to fight in the Middle East, but in the South there is only one "War." Fought between 1861-65, the War Between the States, the War for Southern Independence or the War of Northern Aggression still resonates in our culture. Above is the Daughters of the Confederacy Parade on Main Street circa 1910.

North Carolina was the last state to secede from the Union. It was the firing on Fort Sumter in April 1861 and President Abraham Lincoln's call for troops to put down the "rebellion" that led the Old North State to take this action and join the Confederate States of America.

Men from Surry County and Mount Airy joined and fought for the South during the Civil War in units in their state and across the line in Virginia. Historian Hester B. Jackson wrote that about the beginning of the war starting nearly 9,000 whites and 1,246 slaves in Surry County North Carolina, where Mount Airy occupies the northwest corner. Of these 1,000 men served in regiments such as the 28th, 21st, 53rd, 18th, North Carolina infantry regiments along with regiments such as the 29th, 51st, and 45th Virginia infantry regiments. (Courtesy of the Surry County Historical Society.)

On the following pages are some of the officers who brought the "War" to Mount Airy in April 1865. One of the brigade commanders under George Stoneman who came through Surry County was William Jackson Palmer. Born in Delaware to Quaker parents in 1836, Palmer grew up in Philadelphia before going to work on railroads and traveling to Europe. When war broke out in 1861, he left his church and rose in rank to Brevet Brigadier General. Only George Custer was a younger General in the U. S. Army. Palmer commanded troopers from Ohio, Pennsylvania, and Michigan during the raid and many Surry County residents commented on how well behaved Palmer's men were in comparison to other members of Stoneman's command. Palmer received the Medal of Honor for his service in the war and moved to Colorado after the war, where he built railroads and became a multi-millionaire. At his death in 1909, he had spent millions building churches, schools, and hospitals and founded the city of Colorado Springs. (Courtesy of the Library of Congress.)

Alvin Gillem, a Southerner, commanded the cavalry division under Stoneman during the raid. (Courtesy of the Library of Congress.)

John K. Miller commanded a brigade of cavalry under Stoneman and Gillem. His brigade made up of Southerners took out their feelings on their native section. (Courtesy of the Library of Congress.)

 Simeon Brown commanded a brigade under Stoneman and Gillem during the raid. His men also Southerners were rough on the people of the South. (Courtesy of the Library of Congress.)

 One of the men on the raid was Miles Keogh, an Irishman, who served in the Papal Guard and French Foreign Legion. He lost his life with George Custer in 1876 at the Battle of the Little Bighorn. (Courtesy of the Library of Congress.)

In 1996, this author (above), worked with retired educator Ruth Minick shown below and the North Carolina Department of Historic Resources to place a North Carolina Historical Highway Marker on Rockford Street near the library and across from the Andy Griffith Playhouse.

J. E. B. Stuart (above) while at West Point (1850-54) and below while in the United States Army (1854-61), where he rose to captain. He served in the Kansas Territory, (below) where he encountered Cheyenne Indians and rode the Santa Fe Trail.

Commanding all the cavalry for Robert E. Lee's Army of Northern Virginia (1862-64), Stuart (above and below left) rose to the rank of Major General before one of George Custer's troopers mortally wounded Stuart at Yellow Tavern just north of Richmond in May 1864. Among the men serving with Stuart were four regiments of North Carolina cavalry. (Below right) This author at the site he saved and the sign he wrote replacing the historical marker that started his interest in history. (All Stuart photos courtesy of the author.)

Elizabeth Brown (above left) at Stuart's Birthplace and the 1932 Virginia Highway Historical Marker that began this author's interest in J. E. B. Stuart on the right and the American Civil War. (Below) The 1907 statue of J. E. B. Stuart on Richmond's Monument Avenue.

Grave of Jonathan Hanby Carter in Edgefield, South Carolina, is in the First Baptist Church Cemetery along with Confederate General Matthew C. Butler and Senator Strom Thurmond.

(Above and below) Models of the *CSS Missouri* built under the direction of and commanded by J. H. Carter on the Red River in Louisiana during the last two years of the Civil War.

J. H. Blakemore played in a local brass band and operated a photo studio in Mount Airy after serving in the War Between the States. He took the famous photo of the Siamese Twins. (Courtesy of the Surry County Historical Society.)

The Pennsylvania Monument at Gettysburg, Pennsylvania, includes Mount Airy granite and a statue of Union General John Reynolds, whose mortal wounding is a chapter in this book.

Eng and Change Bunker "The Siamese Twins" above with their wives and oldest son Christopher Wrenn and possibly Steven Decatur Bunker, who served in the Confederate Army, who are also below.

Christopher Wrenn Bunker

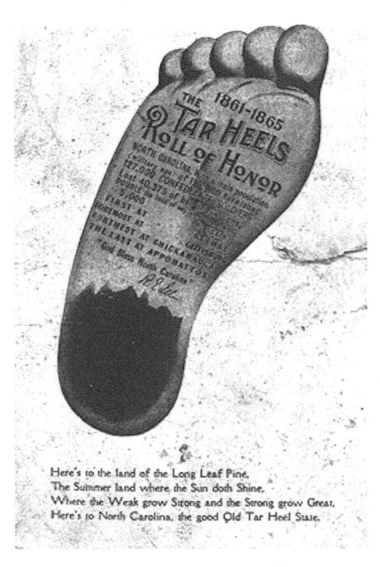

The term Tar Heel has origins in the Civil War and is covered by a chapter in this book.

Lt. Colonel Bazilla Yancy Graves served in the 21st North Carolina Infantry and was the first mayor of Mount Airy in 1885.

Lt. Colonel William Luffman of the 11th Georgia Infantry shot it out with Stoneman's Union Cavalry at Siloam while recuperating from wounds received at the Battle of the Wilderness. He killed one of the Federals before escaping.

Each year in February, Rockford in southern Surry County along the Yadkin River hosts a Civil War Reenactment. This page and the following pages show scenes from the community.

The Mark York Tavern in Rockford has one of the two Civil War Trails signs in Surry County.

89

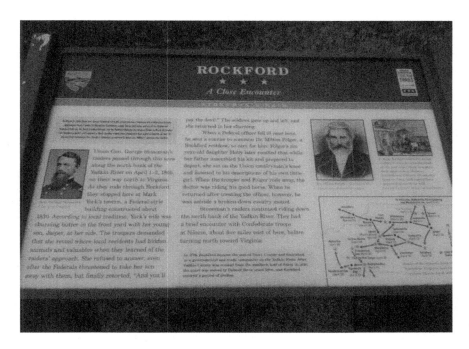

North Carolina Civil War Trails sign at Rockford above and at Siloam below. Both discuss Stoneman's 1865 Raid.

Siloam, in southern Surry County, has a North Carolina Civil War Trails sign that tells of another incident covered in the chapter in this book on Stoneman's Raid.

The marker commemorating the Confederate soldiers from Surry County on this and the next page is at the old Surry County Courthouse at Dobson.

Surry County soldiers are remembered in Mount Airy at the War Memorial those who died in all wars at the corner of Main and Rockford Streets.

Flag of North Carolina denotes date of secession in 1861.

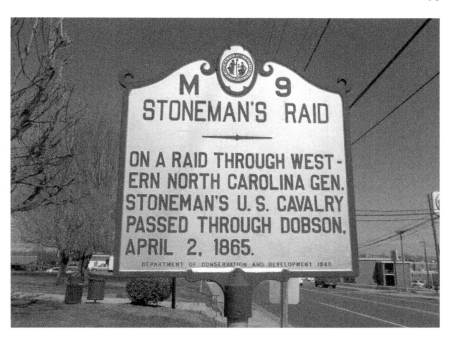

Stoneman's Raid is remembered in Dobson with a North Carolina Highway Historical Marker.

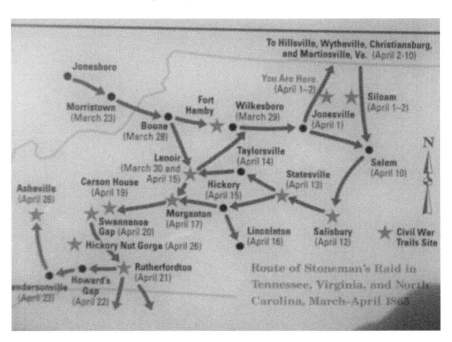

The Siamese Twins are buried at White Plains Baptist Church near their son Steven Decatur, who fought for the South.

Christopher Wrenn Bunker, son of the Siamese Twins is buried at Antioch Baptist Church.

Steven Decatur Bunker is buried at White Plains Baptist Church near the grave of Andy Griffith's paternal grandparents.

Grave of William Norman at Rockford Baptist Church.

Civil War Trails Sign in Elkin, North Carolina

Major Richard E. Reeves retreated with William Luffman at Siloam in April 1865 from Stoneman's Raiders.

Jonathan Hanby Carter served in the United States and Confederates States Navies.

Chapter Four

Jonathan Hanby Carter

In May 1853, J. E. B. Stuart wrote from the United States Military Academy at West Point, New York, to his cousin Bettie Hairston, "A few days ago I had a visit from an old friend and neighbor Jonathan Carter now a Lieutenant in the Navy on the eve of starting out in Ringgold's expedition to Bering's Straights to be absent four years. He looked better than I ever saw him and seemed to anticipate a fine time."

Jonathan Hanby Carter was born on January 1, 1821, in Surry County, North Carolina. His family roots were in Patrick County, Virginia. In 1788, Susannah Hanby (1770-1857), whose father was Jonathan Hanby, married William Carter (1761-1845), the man Historian O. E. Pilson called the "Father of Patrick County." These were Jonathan Hanby Carter's grandparents. William Carter, Jr. (1796-1840) married Elizabeth Moore, a descendant of Rodeham Moore. Jonathan Hanby Carter was their son.

There are still many signs of the Carters in Patrick County. Anytime you travel south from Stuart on Route 8 you will pass

Carter's Mountain on the right just before you reach the intersection with Highway 103 and if you proceed on to Ararat you pass the Carter Cemetery just after crossing the Dan River on the left of the Ararat Highway at the intersection with the Sawmill Road.

The Carter's home still sits on the Old Rail Road, north of Mount Airy and is on the North Carolina and National Registers of Historic Places. It is described as "an outstanding representative of early nineteenth-century Federal-style architecture in Surry County, North Carolina."

The Carters moved from Stokes County to 800 acres on Paul's Creek. The house contains an inscription that says "W C 1834." William died in 1840, preceded a year earlier by Elizabeth Moore Carter.

J. H. Carter began his naval career in March 1840. He served on the *USS Powhatan, USS John Adams, USS Perry, USS Saint Lawrence* and *USS Savannah*. Carter was in the first graduating class at the United States Naval Academy in Annapolis, Maryland, in 1846. He traveled the world rising to the rank of Lieutenant in the United States Navy until the outbreak of war in

1861.

Matthew C. Perry led several expeditions to the Far East to open up China and Japan. Cadwalader Ringgold (1802-1867) led an expedition of five ships beginning in 1853 to survey the western Pacific for the whaling industry. Carter served on the *USS Powhatan* during the expedition.

While traveling the world, Carter kept in touch with his family and roots in Patrick County. The 1859 Patrick County Land Book reports him owning 100 acres worth $100. The Patrick County Deed Book #17 shows him acting as Power of Attorney for two of his brothers the next year.

On April 25, 1861, Jonathan Hanby Carter resigned his commission in the United States Navy and began his second naval career in the Confederate States Navy. His first command involved taking the *Ed Howard*, a side-wheel steamship and turning it into the *CSS General Polk*. The six-gun ship patrolled the Mississippi River and Louisiana coast in the first two years of the war. After fighting in the Battle of Island #10 on the Mississippi River in March 1862, Carter escaped seventy-five miles up the Yazoo River and burned the ship to avoid its capture.

By October, he was building another ship. On November 1, 1862, the Confederate States of America agreed to pay the firm of Moore and Smoker $336,000 to build one ironclad steam gunboat.

Carter found himself in charge of a project that had almost insurmountable problems. He did not let that stop him from completing the work before him. Among these problems were getting the materials and the men to complete the ironclad. A steamboat was purchased for $65,000, but John Pemberton commanding at Vicksburg nearly sank the boat in the Big Black River.

On April 14, 1863, Carter launched the *CSS Missouri* on the Red River near Shreveport, Louisiana. He called it the *Caddo* because of the parish where it was built, but was soon overridden by the Confederate Secretary of the Navy Stephen Mallory five days after the launch. Carter supervised all aspects of its construction including getting local blacksmiths to forge the spikes and bolts.

The ironclad ship carried three guns: one eleven inch, one nine-inch gun and one thirty-two pounder. A Union officer described the ship as "very formidable" but "very slow." Carter's command included 24 officers and 18 men, but it was not very exciting mainly as the low water in the Red River kept the ship from participating in any major campaigns.

The *CSS Missouri* made a trial trip on June 17, 1863, but another problem was discovered. The boat never went faster than ten miles per hour.

Carter became so bored that in February 1864 he wrote, "Feeling desirous of doing my country more effective service I must respectfully request that Steamer Harriet Lane now lying in Galveston harbor be turned over to me for the purpose of running her to some European port and there altering her as to make an efficient cruiser." During the war, he wrote over 262 letters edited by Katherine B. Jeter in *A Man and His Boat: The Civil War Letters of Jonathan H. Carter.*

In March 1864, Union Admiral Porter started up the Red River, but Carter could not respond due to the low water levels. It would be the following year before the river rose enough for the ironclad to move down to Alexandria, Louisiana.

Jonathan Hanby Carter surrendered on June 3, 1865, to Union Lt. Commander Fitzhugh who said of Carter's boat."She is a very formidable vessel, plated with railroad iron resembling the *CSS Tennessee*." He described the boat as having one 11-inch gun, one 9-inch gun, and one 32 pounder. She was "built of green timber, caulked with cotton, leaks badly and is very slow. I do not consider her of any use as an ironclad."

The *CSS Missouri* was the last Confederate ship to surrender in home waters. Union forces sent her to Mound City, Illinois, where she was dismantled and sold for scrap.

After the war, Carter farmed in Louisiana, married Henrietta Tompkins in 1870, and settled near Edgefield, South Carolina, where he died in March 1884. In Edgefield's First Baptist Church cemetery, Carter rests near South Carolina's Civil War Governor Frances Pickens and cavalry General Matthew C. Butler, the man who saved J. E. B. Stuart at Brandy Station in June 1863 bringing this story full circle with relation to J. E. B. Stuart.

Chapter Five

The Siamese Twins and the Civil War

Mark Twain once wrote about the Siamese Twins, Eng and Chang Bunker, who lived near Mount Airy. "During the war they were strong partisans, and both fought gallantly all through the great struggle--Eng on the Union side and Chang on the Confederate. They took each other prisoners at Seven Oaks, but the proofs of capture were so evenly balanced in favor of each, that a general army court had to be assembled to determine which one was properly the captor and which the captive. The jury was unable to agree for a long time; but the vexed question was finally decided by agreeing to consider them both prisoners, and then exchanging them. At one time Chang was convicted of disobedience of orders, and sentenced to ten days in the guard-house, but Eng, in spite of all arguments, felt obliged to share his imprisonment, notwithstanding he himself was entirely innocent; and so, to save the blameless brother from suffering, they had to discharge both from custody--the just reward of faithfulness."

On April 2, 1865, men dressed in blue uniforms approached a house on Stewart's Creek near Mount Airy, North

Carolina. These men from Major General George Stoneman's United States Cavalry were on a mission to draft the two most famous men living in the "Granite City" into the service of the United States. The problem occurred when only one of the men, Chang Bunker, was chosen from the draft lottery, but not his brother, Eng Bunker. Since the two men were conjoined at the abdomen, the Siamese Twins did not ride off to serve in the armies of the United States. It is a great story, but not true. George Stoneman and his over 4,000 Union Cavalry did not need to conscript two Asian-Americans into service.

Before his death on April 15, 1865, Abraham Lincoln did not host the two men from Siam, now Thailand, at the White House either, but it is a good story. Like many stories about these two men, who had three grandparents from China and one from Siam, these Chinese-Americans found themselves in the middle of the War Between the States fought from 1861 until 1865. The war did not visit their homes until April 2, 1865, but they did send at least one of their sons into the Confederate Armies and possibly two.

Born on May 11, 1811, in the Mae Klong Valley, Samut

Songkhram Province, Siam (present day Thailand) to a Chinese father, Ti-aye and a Chinese/Siamese mother, Nok, the brothers were born conjoined thoraopagus twins, the most common form of conjoined twins. They shared part of the chest wall, and their livers were fused.

Siamese King Rama III vacated the decree of death on the boys as they were perceived as evil. At the age of 16, the brothers met their King.

In 1824, Scottish merchant Robert Hunter discovered the twins. After a delay, the government of Siam gave him permission to take them from their homeland. Captain Abel Coffin paid their mother $500 and the twins went on their first world tour of Europe and the United States.

The Bunkers known as "the Chinese twins" in their native Siam, arrived in the United States in 1829. They went out on their own in 1832, working with others including unhappily with P. T. Barnum until they settled down in Wilkes County, North Carolina, in 1839. On October 12, they became naturalized citizens of their adopted country. Four years later, they married sisters Adelaide and Sarah Anne Yates on April 13. These two unions produced twenty-one children.

The Siamese Twins and families moved to Surry County, North Carolina, into two separate homes along the banks of Stewart's Creek by 1852. They returned to touring in 1849 and for over a decade of prosperous living occurred for the Bunker clans until the clouds of war erupted in 1861 with the American Civil War. The war did not touch the Bunkers for two more years when two of their sons came of age and like their fathers embraced the Southern way of life including slave holding.

The first son to fight for the South was born on April 8, 1845. Christopher Wrenn Bunker was the oldest son of either of the Siamese Twins. Named for the famous English architect, Sir Christopher Wrenn (1632–1723), who rebuilt over fifty churches in London after the "Great Fire" of 1666 including St. Paul's Cathedral, Bunker at age 18 in 1863. He enlisted in Company I of the 37th Battalion Virginia Cavalry after traveling over the state line into Virginia, specifically Wytheville.

Chang's oldest son supplied his own horse as was the custom in the Confederate Army. For $12 a month Christopher Wrenn Bunker, found himself not as some thought in "…the idea of the cavalry had been the colored plume in the hat of J. E. B. Stuart, gallant Southern gentlemen astride sleek mounts, and the rustle of the battle flag as they rode across the country side." He found himself in cavalry that one day crossed a creek in waist deep water eight times while riding twenty-two miles or going 100 miles in two feet of snow.

The regiment began with Lt. Colonel Ambrose Dunn of Georgia as "Dunn's Partisans" in August 1862. Reorganized in April 1863, the 37th Battalion Virginia Cavalry became part of William E. "Grumble" Jones command. He led the men through Southwest Virginia, modern day West Virginia and Tennessee. From the Volunteer State, Christopher wrote of his horses. "We had a hard time running of them and they running of us. My horse corked himself and became very lame and I had to leave him with a gentleman who lives five miles this side of Lexington … and if I should get killed or captured on this raid you can send and get him."

Christopher wrote his sister, Nancy, about life in the army in letters now housed in the Wilson Library at the University of North Carolina at Chapel Hill. "About two weeks ago we all went out on a scout and was gone about five days we travelled three nights and days before we made a halt. The second night got me it rained all night as hard as it could pour and we had to travell over the rockyest and the muddyest road that I ever saw and the next morning we ran up on the Yankee pickets and captured them and went on to a little town call Rogersville and there we saw a little fun catching Yankees, we captured about 150 Yankees and started back about twelve o'clock and travelled all night that night and in the whole scout we did not take our saddles off of our horses but once or twice and did not feed but once or twice a day and when we got back to camp every horse in the battalion had the scratches so bad that they could hardly travel."

Jones lost his life at the Battle of Piedmont in June 1864 just before U. S. General David Hunter crossed from present day West Virginia to attack the Shenandoah Valley. Robert E. Lee sent Jubal Early to drive off Union forces under "Black Dave" Hunter from the outskirts of Lynchburg past Hanging Rock near present day, Roanoke, Virginia. Hunter received his sobriquet by commanding African-American troops earlier in the war.

Early then moved north or up the Shenandoah Valley of

Virginia crossing the Potomac River on July 5 into Maryland, Pennsylvania and to the outskirts of Washington, where Abraham Lincoln observed an attack on Fort Stevens on July 11-12.

After moving back into the Old Dominion, Early ordered General John McCausland's brigade of cavalry along with the brigade of Marylander turned Confederate Bradley Johnson to Chambersburg, Pennsylvania. On July 30, 1864, Southern horsemen including Christopher Bunker and the 37th Battalion Virginia arrived in Chambersburg. McCausland promptly demanded a ransom of $500,000 in currency or $100,000 in gold. When he did not receive the ransom, McCausland ordered the town put to the torch.

Lt. Col. Dunn ordered his men to blow up the courthouse and set fire to the adjacent buildings. It is possible that Bunker and his compatriots were involved with this bit of urban renewal as a reaction to Hunter's treatment of Virginia.

The resulting destruction enraged even some of his own subordinate commanders such as Brigadier General Bradley T. Johnson who later wrote, "At Chambersburg, while the town was in flames, a quartermaster, aided and directed by a field officer, exacted ransom of individuals for their houses, holding the torch in terror over the house until it was paid. These ransoms varied from $150 to $750, depending on the size of the habitation. Thus the grand spectacle of a national retaliation was reduced to a miserable huckstering for greenbacks… Every crime in the catalogue of infamy has been committed, I believe, except murder and rape."

McCausland fell back to Moorefield, Virginia, now West Virginia, incorrectly assuming Union forces would not pursue. They did in the guise of Union Brigadier General William V. Averell, who attacked at 3 a.m. on August 7, 1864.

In spite of being outnumbered almost two to one, Averell inflicted a rapid blow on the Southerners. First, the Union forces, some dressed in gray, captured the scouting party sent out to find them and then took the pickets of the Confederate camp. Next, the sleeping regiments of the 1st and 2nd Maryland Cavalry were captured leaving the door open for the rest of the command.

The attack next is the 37th Virginia, who lost more men in this engagement than any other in the war. It was chaos as men retreated across a creek before firing a shot while trying to saddle and bridle their horses with bullets flying all around.

During the melee, Union cavalry shot Christopher Bunker out of the saddle. He became one of twenty-five men from his regiment captured. One only can imagine the shock on the look of the Yankees who captured the very obviously Chinese features of young Bunker.

His horse was later returned to his family near Mount Airy. Christopher found himself a prisoner of war. Bunker was one of the Confederates listed in the Official Records of the War of the Rebellion showing that Averell captured 38 officers and 377 enlisted men in addition to killing at least 13 and wounding 60.

This battle ended the nearly three years of dominance for the Confederates in the Shenandoah Valley of Virginia that began with J. E. B. Stuart and Turner Ashby at Harper's Ferry in 1861. Jubal Early, known for his dislike of cavalry, never had a good record with the mounted arm.

As a guest of the United States, young Bunker soon found himself in the prison at Camp Chase in Columbus, Ohio. The camp originally held only Southern officers, who on their honor of not trying to escape, had free run of the town coming and going as they pleased for the most part even having their slaves serve them.

When Bunker arrived, those days were long gone and officers moved to other camps. The food at Camp Chase was infamous as "gristly slop" and was enhanced by prisoners with rats.

On October 12, 1864, he wrote home. "I was captured the 7th of last August and brought to this place. I have no news of interest to write to you as there are none allowed to come in prison. … I see no chance for an exchange. I have not seen many well days since I came to this place. I have had the smallpox and now got the diareea but I hope that I wil be well in the course of a week. … We are drawing very light rashions here just enough to keep breath and body."

Christopher Bunker survived the smallpox and the diet of rats. He read the Bible when not carving boats or musical instruments. His father sent him money that he used to buy a pocketknife and rations.

Family tradition holds that Eng Bunker's son Steven Decatur Bunker also served in the 37th Battalion Virginia Cavalry. Named for the famous United States Navy officer, Commodore Stephen Decatur (1779-1820), who fought in the War of 1812 and two wars off the coast of African in the Barbary Wars, the first time United States forces encounter Muslims, Steven Decatur Bunker is harder to pin down. Unlike Christopher Bunker, no Compiled Service Record exists for the son of Eng Bunker. A North Carolina Pension Record does exist for him.

Born on March 12, 1846, Steven Bunker turned 18 in 1864, just in time if family tradition is true, to join Christopher in the Confederate Cavalry on July 2. No Compiled Service Record (CSR) survives for Steven in the unit while a CSR for a D. C. Bunker does. It is possible that the clerk got the name confused or maybe misunderstood the accent of the part Chinese cavalryman.

Reportedly present at Moorefield, he was not captured, but later wounded in one of the many battles around Winchester, Virginia, in September 1864, when Philip Sheridan routed Jubal Early ending the Confederate presence in the Shenandoah Valley. The family tradition holds he received another wound in 1865 and was captured before returning home to join his cousin Christopher, where both lived long and fruitful lives receiving pensions for the service of the South.

The 37th Virginia soldiered on before disbanding on April 22, 1865. One of their unit wrote of the end. "With sad hearts we took leave of each other, never to meet again on the battle field. The separation was a sad one, after having been united for so long in the defense of our country, a cause we believed to be right."

Before their returns to Surry County, North Carolina, their fathers, the "Siamese Twins" did encounter Union Cavalry of George Stoneman's raid that began on March 24 at Strawberry Plains near Knoxville, Tennessee, and would not conclude until Confederate President Jefferson F. Davis was captured on May 10, 1865.

On Sunday, April 2, 1865, over 4,000 men on horseback in blue uniforms rode into Mount Airy. George Stoneman, a former roommate of Thomas J. "Stonewall" Jackson at West Point, brought this huge cavalry force in Mount Airy. Arriving as night fell, the Union troopers described Mount Airy as "very ordinary." They helped themselves to letters at the local post office that they "liberated."

The cavalry came all night and into the morning on Monday, April 3, with camps all around Mount Airy. This author suspects the location was along the Ararat River near the present day middle school and possibly along Lovill's Creek as the men and animals needed water.

One trooper Frank Frankenberry got a room at the Blue Ridge Hotel. Word of a wagon train headed up Fancy Gap sent some of the men scurrying north out of town to capture it. Most of the men left the following Monday morning ending the only Union occupation of Mount Airy during the war.

Knowing of the presence of the famous "Chinese Twins," Stoneman ordered his men to leave the family alone. Family tradition holds that one of the Yankee Troopers ignored the order and visited one of the Bunker homes where he grabbed a Bunker daughter and received the only wound the cavalry got that day when he received a slap across the face from the same daughter.

Stoneman's raiders would "Pass the Virginia line and now we are on the sacred soil" of Virginia, where they continued on to places as distant from each other as Wytheville and the Peaks of Otter. Most made it to Christiansburg, where they destroyed the Virginia and Tennessee Railroad before returning through Patrick and Henry Counties back to North Carolina as Robert E. Lee surrendered at Appomattox. They attacked Salisbury on April 12, sacked Asheville and some of the raiders even pursued Jefferson

Davis while most returned to Tennessee.

Eng and Chang Bunker lived until 1874. Steven D. Bunker married Susan Yates and lived on until 1920. Christopher W. Bunker married Mary Haynes and lived on until 1932. In 1879, he got into a financial dispute with his family that did end until the North Carolina Supreme Court sided for him in 1905, which alienated him from his family. The bulk of his estate went to the Baptist Home for Children in Kinston, North Carolina.

Mark Twain in his *Those Extraordinary Twins* might have known the truth better than we realized when wrote about another set of conjoined twins. "At times, in his seasons of deepest depressions, Angelo almost wished that he and his brother might become segregated from each other and be separate individuals, like other men. But of course as soon as his mind cleared and these diseased imaginings passed away, he shuddered at the repulsive thought, and earnestly prayed that it might visit him no more. To be separate, and as other men are! How awkward it would seem; how unendurable. What would he do with his hands, his arms? How would his legs feel? How odd, and strange, and grotesque every action, attitude, movement, gesture would be. To sleep by himself, eat by himself, walk by himself--how lonely, how unspeakably lonely! No, no, any fate but that. In every way and from every point, the idea was revolting."

So, in spite of their own sons fighting for and they themselves supporting their new state of North Carolina. Often tensions frayed the relationship just like the United States of America and the Confederate States of America, Eng and Chang Bunker remained joined together until the end of their time on Earth.

William Norman

Chapter Six

William Norman

On December 23, 1863, William Norman of Surry County began to write down the story of his life. The reason Norman had time to write was that he was a guest of the United States of America as a prisoner of war at Johnson's Island, Ohio, in Lake Erie.

In his memoir titled *A Portion of My Life*, he wrote, "My sole object has been to lay before you the many disadvantages I had to labor under when I entered the theater of my youth and what slow success and advancement I made in education, character, etc. I could not tell you all the pleasures and happiness I used to enjoy when I was blessed with an affectionate mother advice and tender care, before the rambling notions entered my mind."

Born in Surry County, the third son and third child on October 14, 1833, to Clement and Anna Wolff Norman, William Norman, was the only man to write about his experiences in the War Between the States that has been published. John F. Blair in Winston-Salem published the book in 1959 calling it *A Portion of My Life: Being A Short and Imperfect History written while a*

Prisoner of War on Johnson's Island 1864.

In June 1851, Norman lost his mother. Without the consent of his father, William ran away to Hillsville, Virginia, to continue his education. As he left, he turned to look back on the family farm from a high ridge. "Consider a youth of only sixteen summers, with two dollars and a half in money, not a change of clothing complete, without any relatives able to assist him, parents unable to help him, the mortifying thought of only a few months since standing around the deathbed of an affectionate mother, and the idea of going into an entire strange country. This was, I can assure you, enough to make the stoutest heart falter."

Norman did not falter. He attended school and began to teach school. "What portion of a man's life affords him more satisfaction than that of his schoolboy days? The many friends he has an opportunity to make and the pleasant associations which are formed are a source of pleasure to the retired student, even though he may not have enjoyed the opportunity of renewing the associations for many years."

In 1853, Norman was without work and came to a fork in the road on the Blue Ridge Plateau, one leading to the New River and another to Patrick County, Virginia. He flipped a coin and made his way to "the most dark and dismal place I had ever been in." He found a friendly family that "treated very kindly by those poor people."

William felt he was not wise with his money. "It is a great misfortune of young men that, very frequently, when they begin the rough journey of life, they are quite destitute of means. Upon reaching that point when they could accumulate something, they become too free hearted, and having money in their pockets, they choose to spend their money for luxuries instead of investing it in a better and more profitable manner."

In August 1855, Norman went west to Nebraska Territory. He encountered Native-Americans, Pawnees to be exact and spent several years on the frontier.

He returned home to Surry County on May 16, 1858, "very tired and overcome with joy, for I had often thought I would never enjoy the pleasure of seeing my affectionate father any more."

Back home William Norman met Miss Letitia Holyfield. After confiding his love for her, she told him, "If you wish to make me happy and add anything to your own happiness, you must confine yourself to some useful and honorable business and stick to the choice you make until you are able to realize something thereby. Get your mind well settled and call upon me and then you will hear better news."

William Norman did get his mind settled and began to study law with Judge R. M. Pearson in Yadkin County just across the Yadkin River. He received his law licenses and married Letitia Holyfield on March 22, 1860.

With the firing on Fort Sumter in April 1861, Norman foresaw the future. "Everyone knew then that the ball was in motion and that it would require more men to stop it than it took to start it. I often thought of the old adage of 'two men begin a war, but it takes multitudes to stop it.'"

Norman was not comfortable about leaving his new wife. "I have often thought that no one was situated as I was, though there may have been many. I loved my wife; I loved my country. I often asked myself the question, 'Shall I stay at home with my wife and lurk around home, or shall I go and fight for the liberties of my country and how that I am a soldier and willing to resent an injury'"

Norman volunteered on May 4, 1861, in Dobson, for what became Company A, 28th North Carolina Infantry. One hundred and ten men set out for Raleigh at the end of the month. They received training near Weldon at Garysburg along the railroad just south of Richmond. They lost their first men to disease including Samuel Turner, William Bennett, Joseph Riggin, William Ring and Nathan Marion. Disease killed more men than bullets during the war.

Norman made several trips to Raleigh to meet with Governor Ellis and Governor Clark after the former's death. First, he failed to get his men sent to Danville to be with other men from Surry County. Norman received promotion to First Lieutenant. Two more men of the company died, Jeremiah Marion and Joseph Stanley. He then was successful in getting the men moved to High Point.

William Norman became a father on August 26, 1861, when Mary Emma was born. "I felt grateful to God for his kindness in giving me such a present."

The "Surry Regulators" became official on September 21, 1861, at Camp Fisher, High Point, North Carolina, under the command of Captain Richard Reeves. Norman was First Sergeant until Reeves received promotion to captain when Reeves went up to be regimental major. James H. Lane became the colonel of the regiment. On September 30, they arrived in Wilmington, where five more men died.

In 1862, many reenlisted for twelve months. Feeling the need to go home and see his baby daughter and wife, Norman did not reenlist. He had been stricken with chills and fever the preceding fall and was not recovered.

This regiment continued on fighting at New Bern. James H. Lane, a future educator at Virginia Tech was in command for a short time. The regiment saw fighting at Cedar Mountain, Second Manassas, Ox Hill, Sharpsburg, Fredericksburg and Chancellorsville under Thomas J. "Stonewall" Jackson. They fought at Gettysburg after reorganization and by the time of Appomattox, there were eleven men left.

With the reorganization, Norman resigned and went home to be with his family. Recalled to service at the end of 1862, William Norman became a lieutenant in Company A, 2nd North Carolina Infantry.

This unit began in Dobson over a year after Norman originally joined on September 5, 1862. Dr. James Waugh started this unit, the last company from Surry County to join the South. Waugh served as captain until 1863 when Norman took his place after the former died from a mortal wound on May 23, 1863.

William Norman joined his regiment as part of A. P. Hill's Division in Robert E. Lee's Army of Northern Virginia serving in the Second Corps of Thomas J. "Stonewall" Jackson. He saw action at Fredericksburg in December 1862.

The following May, Norman was part of one of the great battles in history at Chancellorsville. On May 1, Norman saw Jackson as he rode by the column. "I know there is a big fight on hand, for I could see it in Stonewall's eyes as he passed by me."

The following day Norman participated in Jackson's flank march. "At daylight on the morning of the 2nd of May we were relieved and went to the rear about one mile to where the roads forked. Here were Generals Lee, Jackson, A. P. Hill, Stuart, and many major generals holding a council of war and planning our attack. Generals Lee and Jackson seemed to be very busily engaged in laying and arranging some broom straws on one end of the box, where some bacon and crackers were placed for their breakfast. At last General Lee gave the straws a stroke and knocked them all off. Rising to his feet and shaking hands with Generals Jackson, A. P. Hill, and some others, he sat down to eat his breakfast, after asking a blessing. General Jackson, I suppose, had already eaten, for he immediately mounted his horse and, uttering a few words to some of his aides, rode off up the road. In a few moments, Jackson's corps was in motion. No one in the ranks knew anything about where we were going but supposed it to be one of Stonewall's flank moments."

Jackson led his men around the flank of the Union Army of the Potomac that day in one of the great military movements in history and William Norman was part of it. Jackson hit and rolled up the Eleventh Corps of the Union Army under the command of Oliver Otis Howard, a friend of J. E. B. Stuart at West Point.

"We continued our march until about three o'clock in the evening, halted, and were give a good long rest time, being in line of battle only for the occasion. Here every man was let into the scene of the moving straws on General Lee's provision box that morning. We learned here, for the first time, that we had succeeded in getting to the rear of the enemy and that they were not apprised of such a move.

The signal was given, and every man rushed to the front as he was commanded. We advanced on the enemy and drove them nearly three miles that evening and during the night. We took a great many prisoners, one battery of four guns, and a great quantity of small arms."

That night Jackson received multiple wounds at the hands of the 18th North Carolina under the command of James H. Lane. J. E. B. Stuart took command of the Second Corps of the army and led it the next day into the history books with one of the greatest victories of Robert E. Lee's career.

The next day, May 3, Norman encountered his previous regiment as he continued on the fight under the command now of Stuart. "We moved forward to the front lines. As we started off, I saw the 28th Regiment and the old company. They gave me a cheer, and forward we all rushed. I got to where the enemy's artillery had been planted on the same morning, but our artillery had drawn up here now, and the fighting yet continued most furiously. At last, about one o'clock, a grand forward movement was made by our troops and the Yankees fled in wild confusion."

"I have never in my life heard the missiles of death whistle so fast and thick around me. I was very nearly covered in the earth many times by bombshells. The bark from the trees often made my face sting, and splinters knocked from the neighboring trees or saplings were stuck in my clothes."

Norman saw the cost of war first hand at Chancellorsville. "Captain Waugh and myself went into the fight with twenty-three men, and all were killed, wounded, or taken prisoners, except myself and one private, of those that went into the fight on Sunday, the 3rd of May." The sights of the battlefield affected even those in command. "General Ramseur had cried like a child when he saw that his brigade was cut up so bad."

"I could not sleep much that night, for the moment my eyes were closed I imagined I could see soldiers falling all around me, and their dying groans rang in my ears all the time. Besides, it was not a mere imagination, for very often during the night we were aroused by the roaring of artillery, but little damage was done."

The next day, May 4, Norman woke to a grizzly scene. "We were surrounded by dead men and horses on all sides. The air was full of the disagreeable stench arising from the decaying dead bodies of the men and horses. They were all buried as fast as could be, but it was impossible to bury them all before they were very much decayed."

On May 10, Thomas J. Jackson died saying, "Let us cross over the river and rest in the shade of the trees." Jackson lost an arm after his own men shot him. He succumbed to pneumonia a week after receiving his wounds.

Norman wrote about Jackson and believed as many still do that if the "Mighty Stonewall" had lived the outcome of the war would have been different. "I should have said something in relation to the death of General T. J. Jackson. His death produced a profound sadness throughout the whole Army of Northern Virginia. Many a soldier who had followed this great general and warrior through the Valley Campaign and the battles around Richmond was filled with sorrow when his death was announced. I hope every man, woman, and child will carefully read the history of General Jackson. When you read the full history of this war after it has ended, you will see that Stonewall Jackson's presence was needed in many a place on the battlefield and on the march after his death. Would to God that we had another Jackson! If Jackson had lived I would not have seen Johnson's Island. But thank God, we yet have good and able leaders in whom our troops have undivided confidence and are willing to spend the last drop of blood upon the altar of their country!"

Norman was present a month later on June 9 when J. E. B. Stuart fought the momentous cavalry battle at Brandy Station in Culpeper County, Virginia. "We remained in camp until early on the morning of the 9th of June. The cavalry had been skirmishing some on the evening and night before. We were ordered down to reinforce them. We got to the battlefield about the time the fight wound up. Our cavalry succeeded in driving the enemy back."

At Gettysburg, Norman and his men fought under Richard Ewell attacking Culp's Hill on the evening of July 2 and the morning of July 3 before the famous Pickett-Pettigrew charge that afternoon. "At dark we were ordered to charge the heights in front of us and dislodge the enemy from his strong position. We moved off by the right flank a short distance and then to the front. We passed our skirmish line and slowly advanced towards the enemy. This was a trying time. The idea of charging strong fortifications in the night time was an awful thing. But everyone was willing to follow our Brigadier General wherever he would lead us. We had undivided confidence in his military skill and patriotism. We drove the enemy's skirmishers and advanced within two hundred yards of the main line of the enemy's breastworks. We got the order then, while we had halted to get ready for a dash upon the enemy, to fall back a short distance. We supposed this was done for the purpose of letting other troops get up even with us, but I learned afterwards that a charge upon the breastworks of the enemy from this point was not contemplated by General Ewell. We retired about one hundred yards, built some protection from the shells of the enemy, and lay in position the balance of the night."

Captured at Kelly's Ford along the Rappahannock River on November 5, 1863, William Norman spent the rest of the war in the custody of the United States. "While we were keeping those in our front from crossing, a portion of our regiment on our regiment on our right and down the river gave way and the enemy crossed at that ford. They came up to our rear, unobserved by us, for our attention was directed to those in our front. Those in our front, seeing we were entirely surrounded, dashed across the river and received a volley from our muskets, when we were ordered to surrender to men in our rear, who we had not seen until this moment...Oh, how I do regret this final occurrence, but such are the fortunes of war!"

An interesting story related to the Norman that has another Mount Airy Connection involves the ancestor of local physician Eric Jarrell. Among the thirteen captured in this unit with William Norman was Albert H. Jarrell. Albert Harvey Jarrell (1835-1923) was born in Rockingham County, North Carolina, and enlisted in Company A, 2nd North Carolina State Troops in Wake County on September 5, 1862. After being captured on May 3, 1863, he was exchanged ten days later only to be captured again on November 7, 1863, near Kelly's Ford, Virginia. He spent several months in prison at Point Lookout, Maryland, before exchanged in February 1865. He married Jane Tickle and lived along the Ararat River on land previously owned by Archibald Stuart. Many of his descendants still live in the area including world famous Bluegrass musician, Tommy Jarrell, and his great-grandson Ararat born and University of Virginia educated, Dr. Eric Jarrell.

One of Jarrell's future neighbors was William Alvis

Mitchell (1838-1915), who hailed from Mississippi. He lost two fingers in the war, but found himself in Company A, 2nd North Carolina State Troops at Appomattox in April 1865 when Robert E. Lee surrendered to U.S. Grant. His copy of Lee's General Order #9 is still a treasured possession of his grandson, William, passed down through his father, John Mitchell.

William A. Mitchell married Lucy C. Taylor (1848-1933), the daughter of Samuel Taylor. William came from Mississippi to Mount Airy to purchase plug tobacco, wagons and mules and then returned to sell the items. On one trip, he met Lucy Taylor at the Blue Ridge Hotel, owned by her father. By 1899, the couple possessed 168 acres along the Ararat River. Between 1900 and 1902, they built a home valued at $200 that was located on the J. E. B. Stuart Birthplace until it was recently torn down. Family tradition states that their son, John, who married Lillie Smith, the daughter of Council and Elizabeth Smith, tore down the buildings adjacent to the structure, which may have dated back to the Stuart time at Stuart's Birthplace or possibly the home of Stuart's great-grandfather, William Letcher, who was killed by Tories in the American Revolution. Mitchell used the materials in the construction of the large white frame house known as the Dellenback-Mitchell House that was part of the preservation of Laurel Hill.

John and Lillie Mitchell had two children. Evelyn, born in 1926 married Ed Richardson and had two children John and Kitty. William Taylor Mitchell, born in 1920, married Maydee Watson. Their two children, Melissa, who married Wesley Collins and then Mike Straka, and Alan Taylor Mitchell, who married Linda Gammons, gave William and Maydee four grandchildren, Chris Collins, Amy Manuel, and Kevin and Randall Mitchell. Their family like many others takes great pride in the connection to Laurel Hill's history.

After first visiting Old Capitol Prison in Washington D. C., Norman found himself at Johnson's Island as a prisoner of war at Sandusky, Ohio, in the middle of Lake Erie on November 14, 1863. "The life of a prisoner of war is a very unpleasant and unhappy life indeed…The despondency of the mind, which covers the soul, cannot be resisted by the unfortunate victim. The thoughts of home, the pleasures and happiness once enjoyed with the loved ones he has been so disagreeably separated from, bring many a tear of sorrow and bring fresh reminiscences of the past to press very heavily upon him, making him feel very unhappy indeed …Immorality prevails to some extent among the prisoners. I have endeavored, however, to keep my mind turned towards God. Often while walking the floor of the prison, I repeat the Lord's Prayer, and I find my whole mind absorbed upon the subject of my future state of existence or my appearing before God."

Released in June 1865, the family tells it took Norman three months to get home. The preface to his book states. "The family tradition is that, when he arrived in Surry County, North Carolina, he was so emaciated that it was possible to run the encircling fingers of one's hand from shoulder to wrist along his arm. Captain Norman never fully recovered his health, nor did he resume the practice of law. He became a small farmer, a surveyor, a justice of the peace, and the father of nine children."

William Norman died in January 1905. He rests today in Rockford Baptist Church Cemetery.

Union General John Reynolds lost his life at Gettysburg.

Chapter Seven

Who Shot John Reynolds?

In 1947, a Mount Airy newspaper article from years earlier told about Pennsylvanian visiting Mount Airy, North Carolina. The visitor specifically visited the granite quarry where the story says the Pennsylvania Monument for the Gettysburg Battlefield was under construction. He was informed that one of the blacksmiths working on the project was the sharpshooter who killed Major General John Reynolds on July 1, 1863, the first day of the battle. The story continues that the man was working on the very statue of John Reynolds for the monument. The Pennsylvanian was introduced to Sharpshooter Frank Wood of the 55th North Carolina Infantry.

The story goes this way. Wood and a Private Cox found themselves separated from their company in a railroad cut, under Yankee fire. After hiding under a rail fence for protection, they saw a Union officer on horseback a few hundred yards away. Wood supposedly heard the officer, standing in his saddle, shouting to his men, "Give them hell, boys, give them the grape!" Cox asked Wood if he could shoot the officer at that distance.

Wood gave it a try, aimed, and fired. The man fell from his horse, and Wood believed it was John Reynolds.

A good story, but easy to debunk. There is no Frank Wood listed on the roster of the 55th North Carolina Infantry, which was the only North Carolina unit engaged at that time of the morning. Reynolds was not with an artillery battery when he was shot. Davis' men did not reach the fence adjoining the railroad cut until the battle was underway for nearly an hour and smoke covered the battlefield making Reynolds almost impossible to see from that area.

So it is possible that Frank Wood killed John Reynolds? Not likely, but the fact that the story is not provable does not take away from the fact that there is indeed a monument of Mount Airy granite with a statue of Reynolds on the battlefield at Gettysburg.

Major General John Reynolds, a Pennsylvanian, turned down command of the entire Union Army of the Potomac just before the Battle of Gettysburg. He was the highest ranking officer killed in the three day Battle of Gettysburg. The monument on the battlefield to the State of Pennsylvania is the largest monument on the field honoring the state that gave the most Federal men, the commander of the Army of the Potomac, George Gordon Meade, and the "Hallowed Ground" that is Gettysburg.

The monument made of Mount Airy granite set over iron and concrete is 110 feet in height and was dedicated on September 27, 1910. The base is lined with bronze tablets listing the Pennsylvania regiments and batteries and the names of over 34,000 Pennsylvanians who participated in the battle. Bronze statues of Pennsylvania generals George Meade, Winfield Scott Hancock, David Birney, Alfred Pleasonton and David Gregg, Governor Andrew Curtin, President Abraham Lincoln and John Reynolds flank each of the arches. There is a staircase that takes visitors to the roof of the monument, where they can see a panoramic view of the battlefield. Topping the dome is the figure of Winged Victory by sculptor Samuel Murray.

Mount Airy, North Carolina, is home to the world's largest open faced granite quarry. Mount Airy granite is now the thing of legend and even myth. The salt and pepper colored stone has made its way all over the world to commemorate those who have passed on such as the Wright Brothers at Kitty Hawk at the Outer Banks of North Carolina or Albert Einstein in Washington, D. C. or to simply supply building material for embassies and bridges.

Mount Airy is the hometown of Andy Griffith, who made the fictional town of Mayberry come to life in the 1960s. Today, if you visit the real Mayberry you can ride around in a squad car that looks just like the one Sheriff Andy Taylor and Deputy Barnie Fife rode. One of the places on the tour will be the quarry in the community of Flat Rock just over the Ararat River from Mount Airy.

Granite is everywhere in Mount Airy. It is in the basement of buildings on Main Street that were built around the formations rather than blast them or cut them out. It is in the middle of the river and in the people's yards, but mostly it is part of the fabric of the community providing jobs and economic benefit for decades and decades to come.

Chapter Eight

Tar Heel

North Carolina Author Thomas Wolfe wrote in November 1930, "Remember the voices of men in Virginia, and the smell of tar in the streets." The Oxford English Dictionary says that "Tar Heel" "is the nickname for a native or resident of North Carolina." Whether a Tar Heel or a Tarheel, the term applies to the people of the "Old North State," but where did it originate?

One myth has it coming from the American Revolution, but this chapter will concentrate on the term and the War Between the States. This legend tells that a group of soldiers from North Carolina in Robert E. Lee's Army of Northern Virginia threatened to put tar on the heels of a group of retreating soldiers, probably Virginians, who were not holding their position in a battle making them honorary Tar Heels. Another story from the Battle of Chancellorsville on May 3 1863, tells of "the brave, chivalric Virginians laying flat on the ground and the 'Tar Heels' whom they so often ridiculed vaulted over them to glory and to victory." Chancellorsville was a great victory for Robert E. Lee's Army of Northern Virginia, possibly the greatest, but at a great cost as

North Carolinians from James H. Lane's 18th North Carolina Infantry shot General Thomas J. "Stonewall" Jackson. Jackson died a week later and was not present at Gettysburg two months later dooming, many believe, the Southern Cause to defeat.

Historian William Powell wrote this about the history of the term and the Civil War. "In a fierce battle in Virginia, where their supporting column was driven from the field, North Carolina troops stood alone and fought successfully. Some Virginians who had retreated asked the victorious troops in a condescending tone, 'Any more tar down in the Old North State, boys?' The response came quickly: 'No; not a bit; old Jeff's bought it all up.' 'Is that so? What is he going to do with it?' the Virginians asked. 'He is going to put it on you'ns heels to make you stick better in the next fight.'"

Some examples from the war follow. "The earliest surviving written use of the term can be found in the diary of 2nd Lieutenant Jackson B. A. Lowrance of the 4th North Carolina Infantry, who wrote the following on February 6, 1863, while in southeastern North Carolina: "I know now what is meant by the Piney Woods of North Carolina and the idea occurs to me that it is no wonder we are called 'Tar Heels.'"

It was not just the Virginians, who mocked the men from North Carolina. The state is known as a valley of humility between two mountains of conceit, a humorous reference to Virginia and South Carolina. Virginia saw most of the fighting east of the Blue Ridge Mountains. South Carolina started the war with secession and the firing on Fort Sumter at Charleston in 1861. South Carolinian Lt. R. H. Bacot commanding the *CSS Neuse* wrote of his crew for the ship named for a Tar Heel river "to complete our misery we have a crew of long lank Tar Heels."

In the third volume of *Walter Clark's Histories of the Several Regiments from North Carolina in the Great War, 1861 to 1865*, published in 1901, James M. Ray of Asheville relays another story. During the Battle of Murfreesboro or Stone's River as the Union men called it in Tennessee in 1863, General John S. Preston of Columbia, South Carolina, rode in front of the 60th North Carolina Regiment, praising with, "This is your first battle of any consequence, I believe. Indeed, you Tar Heels have done well." Another mention was "Now Tar Heels when you get out yonder clap your foot down and stick."

The earliest printed use of the term comes from a song

"Wearing of the Grey," a Confederate war song that mentioned Tar Heel in 1866 as the composer. North Carolina Governor Vance said in a speech to the troops during the war in Virginia. "I do not know what to call you fellows. I cannot say fellow soldiers, because I am not a soldier, nor fellow citizens, because we do not live in this state; so I have concluded to call you fellows Tar Heels."

The term was not always a positive. Two years later in 1868, Stephen Powers reported that "You see, sir, the Tar-heels haven't no sense to spare," Powers quotes the sergeant as saying. "Down there in the pines the sun don't more'n half bake their heads. We always had to show 'em whar the Yankees was, or they'd charge to the rear, the wrong way, you see." An African-American Congressman from South Carolina said of his white neighbors to the north, "the class of men thrown up by the war, that rude class of men I mean, the 'tar-heels' and the 'sand-hillers,' and the 'dirt eaters' of the South - it is with that class we have all our trouble." "The *Encyclopedia Britannica*, which reported that the people in 1884 who lived in the region of pine forests were "far superior to the tar heel, the nickname of the dwellers in barrens."

The New York Tribune further differentiated among North Carolinians on September 20, 1903, when it observed, "the men really like to work, which is all but incomprehensible to the true 'tar heel.'"

In August 1869, a San Francisco magazine, *Overland Monthly*, published an article citing a number of slang terms for the Old North State. One told of a North Carolina brigade at Chancellorsville who "failed to hold a certain hill, and were laughed at by the Mississippians for having forgotten to tar their heels that morning."

During the war, many negative examples come down to us. Michael W. Taylor in his pamphlet published by the North Carolina Department of Historical Resources wrote, "When the lank and lean denizens of the North Carolina piney woods began to pour into Virginia in 1861 as soldiers in the Confederate army, their crude and humble appearance inspired some waggish Virginia soldiers to call them 'Tar Heels.'"

Eventually the term began to have a positive meaning. In 1893, the University of North Carolina named its newspaper *The Tar Heel*. The athletic teams at the school in Chapel Hill still carry the moniker, which began with the football team around 1926. They stopped being the "White Shadows," a not very politically correct reference to the Klu Klux Klan, to become the Tar Heels.

Of course, the term comes from the production of naval stores. Tar, pitch, and turpentine came from the forests of pine trees. Historian William Powell noted, "For several years before the American Revolution, the colony shipped more than 100,000 barrels of tar and pitch annually to England." Some historians believe that North Carolina from 1720 to 1870 was the world's largest producer of these naval products. Pine tar was the caulking that sealed the hulls of wooden ships.

The process was "messy and smelly." It involved stacking pine logs, covering them with earth and setting them on fire causing tar to run "through channels dug on the lower side of the pile." The people of North Carolina became "Tarboilers." Even poet Walt Whitman wrote, "the people of North Carolina were called 'Tar Boilers.'" These terms were not positive and instead of the Old North State, North Carolina was the "Tar and Turpentine State."

There is no written mention of Tar Heel before the Civil

War. Everything, at least in this book, comes back to the Civil War. A Mister Hancock of Raleigh wrote Senator Marion Butler in 1899, to "commend him for his efforts to obtain pensions for Confederate veterans. This was an action, Hancock wrote, 'we Tar Heels, or a large majority of us, do most heartily commend.'"

One of my favorite stories involved the 4th Texas Infantry who lost their flag at the Battle of Sharpsburg, Maryland, or Antietam as the Yankees called it. As the Texans passed by the 6th North Carolina, the Texans jeered their fellow Southerners yelling, "Tar Heels!" The North Carolinians replied, "If'n you had had some tar on your heels, you would have brought your flag back from Sharpsburg."

Another involving the Battle of Chancellorsville involves some Tar Heels responding to some mocking men from Mississippi in May 1863. "Yes damn you. If yer hader had some tar on yet own heels yestiddy yer would er stuck to them that works better, and we wouldn't er had to yer back thar."

One thing that all Civil War students know is that when in doubt give the credit to General Lee. Colonel Joseph Engelhard, described the Battle of Ream's Station, Virginia, "It was a 'Tar

Heel' fight, and ... we got Gen'l Lee to thanking God, which you know means something brilliant."

The *Grandfather Tales of North Carolina History* from 1901 states that: "During the late unhappy war between the States it [North Carolina] was sometimes called the 'Tar-heel State,' because tar was made in the State, and because in battle the soldiers of North Carolina stuck to their bloody work as if they had tar on their heels, and when General Lee said, 'God bless the Tar-heel boys,' they took the name."

There was no company or regiment that used the name Tar Heel at the beginning of the war, but by the end of the "late unpleasantness", many embraced the name. Governor Zeb Vance might have said it best. "The troops from North Carolina can afford to appeal to history. I am confident that they have but little to expect from their associates."

Chapter Nine

Stoneman's 1865 Raid

This story begins for me one hundred years after the end of the war with Elizabeth Prescott Hobbs making chicken and dumplings from scratch in her home on Fenwick Street in Augusta, Georgia. My grandmother "Momma Lizzie" used to tell me, her youngest grandchild, stories while we kneaded out the dough on her dining room table the day before my mother's family met for our annual Thanksgiving feast. One story she loved to tell was how her family had to hide the silver when William T. Sherman marched through Georgia arriving in Savannah by Christmas 1864.

One thing we always hear about Sherman is the story repeated by almost every family of hiding valuable from the hordes of Yankee plunderers. This was my introduction to the Civil War. For Southerners, this war is part of our psyches from a very young age or as Faulkner said for every young boy in the South it is the afternoon of July 3, 1863, Pickett and Pettigrew's men have not yet charged up Cemetery Hill at Gettysburg and there is still a chance for victory. Southerners feel this war in a way unknown to people who came to this country after the war or who move into the "New

South." I think this goes back to defeat of the Confederate armies and living through the harshness of Reconstruction. We should never forget that Southerners were the first Americans to lose a war.

In the early 1990s, my phone rang and Ruth Minick was on the other end, a retired educator and local historian, who wrote a weekly article for the Mount Airy News. Like many others, Ruth allowed me to see her historic archive that required crawling under beds to pull out boxes. She asked me to assist her working with the North Carolina Department of Historic Resources to place a long approved historic marker in Mount Airy. The topic of that marker was Stoneman's Raid. Ruth wanted it placed along South Main Street near Hamburg Street, where she thought Stoneman's men camped down in the bottom along the Ararat River. We did not get our way on the location. The marker today sits in front of the library on Rockford Street across the street from the statues of Andy and Opie making their way to the fishing hole.

Appalachian State University professor Ina Van Noppen wrote a short book in 1960 later reprinted in the North Carolina Historical Review that covered the raid for five decades. While preparing this article, I mentioned within earshot of my father, Erie

Perry, the name Van Noppen. He then relayed the ironic information that as a student at Appalachian State University he lived in the Van Noppen basement while she researched Stoneman's Raid. Chris Hartley's definitive *Stoneman's 1865 Raid* came out in 2010 and will no doubt be the best work on the subject for decades to come.

I make it a practice to search the Internet about topics I give talks on or articles I write. Recently, I did this for Stoneman's Raid and discovered in the late 1960s, Robbie Robertson of The Band wrote a song that began with this verse: "Virgil Caine is the name and I served on the Danville train Till Stoneman's cavalry came and tore up the tracks again. In the winter of '65 we were hungry, just barely alive. By May the tenth, Richmond had fell, it's a time I remember oh so well *The Night They Drove Old Dixie Down...*"

This song could be a metaphor for the darkness of a crushing defeat or the chorus could be the jubilation of the northern people in victory. It could be simply discussing the fortnight at the end of March and beginning of April 1865 that ended the Civil War. This is an obscure action in relation to the over 10,000 engagements fought between 1861 and1865 mentioned one hundred years later in a song.

The first question might be who are they who drove old Dixie down? The men who brought the Confederate States of America to its knees were the President of the United States, Abraham Lincoln, the General-In-Chief, Ulysses S. Grant and his subordinate General William T. Sherman. In late March 1865, these three men met at City Point, near Petersburg, Virginia. Lincoln recently inaugurated for a second term, Grant laying siege to Richmond, Petersburg and Robert E. Lee's Army of Northern Virginia, and "Uncle Billy" Sherman had just defeated the remnants of the Army of Tennessee under Joseph E. Johnston at Bentonville, North Carolina.

These men wanted to break up the remaining armies of the south especially Lee and Johnston and keep them apart. This included destroying anything that assisted the Confederate war effort to fight and to a degree to bring the war to the areas so far untouched by war. Lincoln said it best to Sherman, "All I want of you is to defeat the rebel armies and get the Confederate soldiers back on the farm." He did not particularly care if Jefferson Davis, President of the CSA got away or not, possibly wishing to avoid the issue of secession in a court of law.

A superficial look at a map will show you that what was left of the Confederacy was a box of land from Richmond west to Tennessee, south to North Carolina and across to Raleigh where Sherman was moving. Near Knoxville, Tennessee, a Union general waited for his chance to pay back the Confederates. His name was George Stoneman.

George Stoneman's raid through our region in the spring of 1865 was the only action our region saw during the War Between The States. Let us start with a short bio about General Stoneman and then talk about the raid in the context of the total war in March through May of 1865.

Major General George Stoneman was born on August 22, 1822 in Busti, now Lakewood, New York, to George and Katharine Aldrich Stoneman. Named for an uncle killed in the British Army in the Battle of the Nile in Egypt, Stoneman attended Jamestown Academy where he was described as "a correct moral man." He attended the United States Military Academy at West Point in the heralded class of 1846 that included George B. McClellan, Jesse L. Reno, Darius Couch, Samuel Sturgis, Cadmus Wilcox, and George Pickett. During his third year, Stoneman's roommate was a poor orphan from western Virginia. A cadet described Thomas J. Jackson and Stoneman as "such quiet neighbors I scarcely knew they were there." After graduating 33rd in a class of 59, the six foot four inch Stoneman, a "generous hearted, whole souled companion" went west. During the Mexican war Stoneman was part of a march from Kansas to California in the Mormon Battalion. He fell in love with the state and vowed to make it his home one day.

U.S. Secretary of War, Jefferson Davis, appointed Stoneman to the Second United States Cavalry. His commanding officers included Colonel Albert Sydney Johnston, Lt. Colonel Robert E. Lee and Major George H. Thomas. In 1861, serving in the 2nd U. S. Cavalry in Texas, Stoneman called the "Lone Star State" a "god forsaken country…I will embrace the first opportunity to get to California and it is altogether probable that when once there I shall never again leave it." In 1861, Stoneman refused to surrender to Confederate authorities and took part of his command and escaped north via ship.

He served under his former West Point classmate, McClellan in the early part of the war. He married Mary O. Hardisty of Baltimore in November 1861. The couple had four children.

Stoneman led the First Division of the Third Corps during the Peninsula and Seven Days campaigns. He commanded an infantry Corps at Fredericksburg. He received promotion to Brigadier General in August 1862 and Major General in November. On "Jeb" Stuart's thirtieth birthday, February 6, 1863, "Fighting Joe" Hooker commanding the U. S. Army of the Potomac reorganized the cavalry corps and placed Stoneman in command. During Chancellorsville in May 1863, Stoneman left Hooker blind while raiding towards Richmond and became the scapegoat of the Union defeat. Using medical problems as a reason, specifically hemorrhoids, Stoneman ran a cavalry bureau near Washington, D. C.

On May 12, 1864, the day J. E. B. Stuart died in Richmond Stoneman was in Georgia taking command of Sherman's left during the Atlanta Campaign. In an effort to redeem his reputation, Stoneman and 2000 cavalry went on a raid to free the Union soldiers at Andersonville. Sherman told him that if successful it would be "an achievement that will entitle you, and the men of your command, to the love and admiration of the whole country." On July 31, 1864, Stoneman along with 700 of his men became prisoners while raiding towards Andersonville. This made him the highest ranking Union general captured during the war.

Exchanged in September 1864, Stoneman presented a plan to his immediate commander and friend, Major General John M. Schofield. Expressing that, "I owe the Southern Confederacy a debt I am very anxious to liquidate," Stoneman's plan called for a two-phase attack on the railroad in southwest Virginia and the Confederate munitions factory at Salisbury, North Carolina.

The U. S. Secretary of War referred to Stoneman as "one of the most worthless officers in the service." Before a communication from the War Department relieved him from duty for his poor performance in Georgia, Stoneman set off to complete phase one to rousing success in December 1864. Schofield convinced Grant to revoke the dismissal order. Stoneman raided into Southwestern Virginia, where he took 4 towns, 900 prisoners, 19 cannons, 3,000 horses and "four pestiferous secession printing presses."

An interesting sidelight to the raid on Saltville in December 1864 was the presence of Mrs. J. E. B. Stuart in the community with her two children after her husband's death. Young "Jeb" Stuart, Jr.

heard gunshots and thinking that firecrackers were going off proceeded to investigate. Flora Stuart stopped the charge of young Stuart on Stoneman before any damage occurred on either side. Another story about this raid involves a Yankee trooper admiring a portrait of Archibald Stuart. When the Yankee learned that it was indeed the father of Lee's dead cavalryman, he slashed the picture with his sword. The painting still displays its battle scar. After an encounter with Jeb Stuart, Jr. and the portrait of Archibald Stuart, Stoneman's raid on Saltville restored his reputation and opened the way for phase two and the road to Patrick County.

In early 1865, Stoneman found himself commanding the Department of East Tennessee under the command of George H. Thomas. A native Virginian, Thomas, the "Rock of Chickamauga" was in Command of the Department of the Cumberland headquartered in Nashville.

With U.S. Grant surrounding Petersburg and Richmond, William Sherman moving through the Carolinas, Stoneman left Tennessee on a raid that would carry him through North Carolina, and into Southwest Virginia and back into North Carolina. George Thomas told Stoneman to "dismantle the country to obstruct Lee's retreat." General Grant told him to "leave nothing for the rebellion to stand upon." He wanted to free the prisoners at Salisbury and to "destroy, but not to fight battles." They intended to "throw the burden of the war on the disloyal citizens of the revolted province," but "all robbery, pillaging, sacking, rape, wounding, maiming, etc are prohibited."

General Alvan C. Gillem led his Cavalry Division of three brigades. Born in Gainesboro, Tennessee. In 1830, he attended a military academy in Nashville with future Confederate Brigadier General Laurence S. Baker. Gillem graduated from the United States Military Academy at West Point, New York, in 1851. At Mills Springs in 1862, Gillem acted as Quarter Master for George Thomas. The next year Andrew Johnson appointed him Adjutant General for the "the Volunteer State." A promotion to Brigadier General came in August 1863. In January 1865, forces of the "able but ruthless" Gillem killed the famous Confederate cavalry raider John Hunt Morgan.

Colonel William J. Palmer led the First Brigade of cavalry including the Tenth Michigan Cavalry Regiment under the command of Colonel Luther Trowbridge, the Twelfth Ohio under

Colonel Robert H. Bentley and the Fifteenth Pennsylvania under Lieutenant Colonel Charles M. Betts.

Palmer, born a Quaker in 1836 in Delaware, grew up in Philadelphia and served as a railroad engineer before the war. During the Maryland Campaign of 1862, Confederates captured Palmer and imprisoned him at Castle Thunder in Richmond. After being exchanged, he served in the campaigns of Tullahoma and Chattanooga in middle Tennessee during 1863. One commander said Palmer was worth "a whole brigade of most cavalry."

Brevet Brigadier General Simeon Batcheldor Brown led the Second Brigade consisting of the Eleventh Kentucky under Major Frederick Slater, the Twelfth Kentucky under Major James B. Harrison and the Eleventh Michigan under Lieutenant Colonel Charles E. Smith. Brown, born and educated in New Hampshire, worked in the private sector before and after the war as a merchant, farmer and hotel owner.

Colonel John K. Miller commanded the Third Brigade, including the Eighth Tennessee under Colonel Samuel K. N. Patton, the Ninth under Colonel Joseph H. Parsons and the Thirteenth Tennessee under Lieutenant Colonel Brazilliah P.

Stacy. These men of the second and third brigades, described by Stoneman as "a fine body of Cossacks," caused many problems during the raid. Miller, born and raised in Carter County, Tennessee, served as Sheriff before the war and organized the 13th Tennessee Cavalry.

Battery E of the First Tennessee Light Artillery under Lieutenant James M. Regan (four guns with caissons) and a detachment of Signal Corps under Second Lieutenant Theodore Mallaby, Jr. completed the Union force. The Ninth Tennessee did not accompany Stoneman on the raid. Also, on the raid were one wagon, four ambulances and two pack mules (one for ammunition, one for the men's mess.)

Sherman had gone from Tennessee to Atlanta in September 1864. He left the city with 62,000 men on his "march to the sea" and entered Savannah on December 21 after inflicting 100 million dollars damage. On January 19, 1865, he left Georgia for South Carolina with 100,000 men. On February 17, Columbia burned and Charleston evacuated, leaving the state that started the war totally at the mercy of Sherman. His army continued north towards North Carolina at a pace of 10 miles a day whether it rained, whether it was through swamp, or whether it had to build bridges, Sherman kept moving north reaching North Carolina on March 8, 1865.

On March 21, William Sherman and Joseph Johnston finished fighting a three day battle at Bentonville, North Carolina, with over 4,000 casualties. These men had fought from 1862 along the Ohio and Mississippi rivers and, now, Sherman with an overpowering force of nearly 100,000 men against a Confederate army of 20K had fought their last battle.

On March 21, 1865, Stoneman with 4,500 men left "Strawberry Plains" at Mossy Creek, Tennessee. One trooper wrote, "We started from Knoxville in an ordinary rain storm which increased in intensity during the day, and at night had developed into a furious hailstorm."

On March 23, 1865, Stoneman reached Morristown, Tennessee. He gave his men five days rations, one-day forage of corn, four horseshoes with nails and sixty-three rounds of ammunition. The local citizens in pro-Union East Tennessee received the raiders with open arms. In fact, Andrew Johnson, who succeeded Abraham Lincoln as President of the United States, lived in the area.

Word of the approaching Yankee cavalry caused many Southerners to hide money, jewelry, food and clothing. One civilian described it as "the biggest burying I ever attended." On a pass near Stone Mountain one trooper wrote, "Our march this night was one that those who participated in it will never forget. The road at times ran close to dangerous precipices over which occasionally a horse or mule would fall...Many loyal citizens built fires along the road and at dangerous places and at difficult fords over the mountain streams."

The suffering of the pro-Union people made an impact on one local man. "My vocabulary is too limited to attempt a portrayal of the horrors and sufferings of those poor Union people...monarchy and ruin reigned supreme; men and neighbors who had always passed as good men...were transformed into demons, murderers and savages. Conscripts were hunted down like wild animals and often shot and murdered."

Stoneman reached Boone, North Carolina, on March 28. Forced to attack the Home Guard, his command killed nine and captured 68 men. Leading the attack was Captain Miles Keogh with a detachment of the 12th Kentucky Cavalry. Keogh, born in

Ireland, served in the French Foreign Legion in Africa and as a Papal Guard in Italy, but lost his life on June 25, 1876, with George Custer's command along the banks of the Little Bighorn River in Montana.

They plundered several homes and burned the local jail. Stoneman accompanied Palmer and the artillery through Deep Gap to Wilkesboro. The other brigades traveled through Flat Gap to the county seat of Wilkes, North Carolina's most unionist county. These units burned Patterson's Mills near Boone, which had supplied other Yankee troops. Gillem did not recognize neutrality among the Southerners saying the "government had been too lenient and rebels must look out for consequences." Stoneman rebuked him for this action.

Brigadier General Davis Tillson commanding the 4th Division guarded the mountain passes with pro-Union infantry and artillery from North Carolina, Tennessee, and Kentucky along with Ohio men and the 1st U. S. Colored Heavy Artillery.

They reached Wilkesboro the next day. During the occupation, they seized the horse of Confederate General James B. Gordon and paraded it around in front of the dead general's home.

Gordon served in Stuart's cavalry and died a few days after him in May 1864. Another sad incident was the death of Jacob Council in Watauga County, killed by Union troopers after one of his slaves referred to him as an "infernal rebel." Gillem's "homegrown" troops received credit for these incidents and the burning of the Boone jail. Stoneman's raiders from the North were well behaved. The exceptions were the "homegrown Tennesseans" and Kentuckians regiments of the second and third brigades. These units wanted to wreak vengeance on their Southern brethren.

    The flooding Yadkin River separated Palmer's men, who crossed to the north side, from the remainder of the force on March 29. One trooper said, "the very heavens…opened their flooding gates." Stoneman, south of the river, ordered a review of the remainder of the forces. The resulting review in the rain revealed the pillaging by Gillem's men as large numbers of men riding in stolen carriages and even a stagecoach, its drivers fortified by Wilkes County moonshine, passed by. Stoneman reportedly "roared like a lion" and demoted officers on the spot. One officer in describing the commanding general said, "Swearing does not look well in print."

On April 1, Stoneman's command still divided by the Yadkin River reached Elkin in Surry County, North Carolina, on the north side of the river and Jonesville on the south side respectively. They found sixty flirty girls working in a cotton mill in Elkin. The Union soldiers put the girls and two other mills to work grinding meal for the "Yankee boys." Stoneman sent Palmer's men full of honey, molasses, butter, chestnuts and smoking cigars down the river to trick the Confederate leaders on "All Fool's Day" that the raid was headed for Salisbury.

Near Petersburg, Phillip Sheridan broke the back of Robert E. Lee's Army of Northern Virginia at Five Forks. Lee's lines extended over 35 miles with fewer men and fewer supplies was at the breaking point. The next day U. S. Grant attacked all along the lines.

Stoneman reunited his entire command on the north side of the river in Surry County at Rockford on April 2. P. G. T. Beauregard, then in command of Western North Carolina had a large force at Salisbury and could have repulsed Stoneman. Instead, the Yankee Cavalry made a diversion toward Virginia that led them to the Virginia Tennessee Railroad at Christiansburg.

A native of Surry County, James Gwyn, commented on the Yankee raiders as they came by his place on the north side of the Yadkin. "The Yankees passed along on both sides of the river. We were all agreeably disappointed. Those who passed acted very well. Indeed, only taking cattle, horses and mules and did not even enter our houses or do violence to our families and destroyed nothing, but a little corn and oats. Treatment of citizens by Palmer's Brigade on the north side of the river evoked the surprise of the residents who feared much harsher treatment."

Another Gwyn saved his tobacco factory by giving the Union men all the tobacco they wanted. One little girl got angry with another Federal, who stopped to play with her doll reminding him no doubt of his own daughter.

Not everyone in Surry County that spring felt the same way about Stoneman and his cavalry. At Rockford, which from 1789 until 1853 was the county seat of Surry County before it was moved to Dobson, Mark York's wife was churning butter with her young son. Federals reportedly threatened to take the boy if she did not reveal where animals and valuables were hid. She warned the cavalrymen, "And you'll pay the devil." The Yankees backed down to Mrs. York.

Federals summoned Dr. Milton Folger. His daughter reported that her father left on a good horse and returned on a "broken down cavalry mount."

Lt. Colonel William Luffman of the 11th Georgia Infantry was recuperating from wounds received at the Battle of the Wilderness in May 1864 at the home of the Reeves family in Siloam.

Luffman of Spring Place, Georgia, north of Atlanta, was born on November 1, 1820. He joined the Confederates on July 3, 1861, as Captain of Company C of the 11th Georgia Infantry. He received promotion to major in January 1862 and four months later in May he became Lieutenant Colonel. Serving in James Longstreet's First Corps of the Army of Northern Virginia under Robert E. Lee, Luffman received a wound in his hip on May 7, 1864.

The Mount Airy News of November 11, 1897, reported "one of the fiercest battles of the late Civil War" by W. M. Cundiff. While bathing in the office of the Reeves family, that is the only building still standing from the time, Luffman found his bath interrupted stating, "Great Heavens, Major, the Yankees are upon us." The Georgian grabbed his "carbine" and went out the door, where a Union Cavalryman demanded his surrender from the back of Luffman's own horse appropriated from the stable. Luffman replied, "This is my gun and I have a perfect right to use it; besides, I see you are on my horse; get off at once or I'll help you off!" The Yankee replied, "Damn you surrender!" Luffman replied with a shot from his gun that killed the cavalryman.

Major Reeves joined in firing his double barrel shotgun. The two Southerners found themselves facing "five hundred Federals arrayed in deadly combat with only two Confederates!" The two men emptied a carbine, two shotguns and four revolvers.

"Major Masten" of the Union ordered a charge against the office. Feeling that retreat was their only option, Reeves and Luffman "turned their faces towards the friendly river" still wearing their night clothes as bullets "whizzed all around them."

John Hardy, age 18, a worker on the Reeves's farm fled, but surrendered. George "a colored man" saved the young man's life by convincing the "Yanks" that Hardy was not involved.

Luffman and Reeves reached the river and hid in the

"weeds and briars" breathing "only through their noses" above water avoiding fifty cavalryman. Reeves later found the Georgia Colonel "clinging to an overhanging branch." The two men escaped to Salem, North Carolina, got some clothes and continued on to Davidson County.

Stoneman's men began to burn the Reeves home, but Major Reeves's mother, Elizabeth Early Reeves, saved her home by promising to bury the dead Union cavalryman, which she did just north of the house. Luffman returned to Georgia, where he died on December 13, 1893.

On April 2-3, Robert E. Lee and the Army of Northern Virginia evacuated Richmond and Petersburg. Brigadier General John Echols in command of Confederate forces in Southwestern Virginia had 4, 000 infantry and 2,200 cavalry spread out across Southwest Virginia but was more concerned with joining Lee than fighting Stoneman. Echols ordered a concentration at Christiansburg. Stoneman's raiders moved through Dobson "not a very pretentious village" to Mount Airy.

The Yankees described the future birthplace of Andy Griffith as the "home of the famous Chinese (Siamese) twins, Eng and Chang, who after exhibiting themselves through Europe and this country and accumulating a large fortune married two ladies who were sisters, and built them an elegant home and settled down in this little Southern town." The Yankees raided the Mount Airy post office and read the letters for days afterward. While camping on the banks of the Ararat River, the men learned of a supply train that had just passed through on its way to Hillsville, Virginia. A pursuit ended after several days with the capture and burning of seventeen wagons. A letter between two sisters, the daughters of Robert Hines, in North Carolina at this time captures the local feeling of this event from Mount Airy.

"Dear Sister,

    I thought that I would write you a few lines. I know you would be uneasy. Sister, the Yankees have been here. They say there was seven thousand, but I don't know how many there was but it was the most men I ever saw and some say ten thousand but I don't know how many there was but it was the most men I ever saw in all my lifetime since they were all Cavalry. Oh Sister you never saw the like in your life. There said to be four brigades. They comensed coming about dark Sunday night and kept coming most all night. Most all the men in town left and run to the woods. Will and Uncle Yancey and Uncle Frank left but Will staid until he saw them coming. One rode his horse here to Pateses, and Will said Mr. Wil was standing in the road talking and he told Will to halt. He jumped over the fence and run and I did not see him any more until Monday evening but the town was not clear of them until Monday evening at sundown. I don't begin to tell you all they done. I have to weight (wait) until I see you. The plundered Uncle Frank's house and took Will's and Uncle Frank's clothes all Will's but what he had on and Sall hid his shoes and we did not know anything about it. The Negros done remarkable well hardly any from this neighborhood went with them. They plundered Aunt Matt's house but she was here this evening and said tell you that she was alive yet. I did not faint or get sick. I was not scared near as bad as I thought although we had two right good Yankees to come in. We got supper for them. Will got a horse from the Yankees to pay for his clothes. They did not plunder our house a tall. They all send their love. Give m love all and write soon to your affectionate sister."

Stoneman's four thousand men camped around Mount Airy on the night Robert E. Lee evacuated Richmond, Virginia, the Capitol of the Confederate States of America. The camping spots reportedly included the site of Veteran's Park along Lebanon Street and the bottomland along Lovill's Creek. Another was the Old Rail Road near Piper's Gap and the Wash Cox place at Green Hill near present day Cross Creek Country Club. This author believes that the primary camp was near the home of Jacob Brower along the Ararat River as Brower was a known Unionist and Stoneman would surely gravitate to the most prominent Union man in Mount Airy.

Theodore Mallaby of the Signal Corps wrote in his report: "April 3rd moved at 5 a.m.; crossed Blue Ridge Mountains through Fancy Gap; halted at Hillsville, Virginia at 1 p.m." Stoneman sent Colonel Miller and five hundred men from the Third Brigade to Wytheville to destroy two railroad bridges over Reedy Creek. Miller ran into Confederates under the command of General John C. Vaughn and Colonel Henry Giltner. Miller lost thirty-five men and rejoined the command at Taylorsville, now Stuart, by returning through Hillsville.

Colonel Miller's men made their way to Patrick County via Hillsville on April 8. One of them reported, "During the night some of the men found two barrels of brandy and after the 'spirits' went down the men's spirits went up and many men and officers began to get merry," The merriment ended when an officer opened the barrels and left the contents on the ground.

The rest of the raiders crossed the Blue Ridge Mountains at Fancy Gap, met slight resistance from the Home Guard and entered Hillsville on April 3. The remainder of the force moved to Jacksonville, now Floyd. They arrived on April 4 at noon.

Gillem's Reports states: "After feeding in the vicinity of Hillsville the march was resumed at sunset in the direction of Jacksonville. Shortly after dark our advance came upon a force of rebels, which was charged and driven several miles. At 12 a.m. the command bivouacked in the vicinity of a tithe depot of hay. The march was resumed at daylight on the morning of the 4th, and arrived at Jacksonville at 10 a.m. where another tithe depot of hay and corn furnished an ample supply for our animals."

Two citizens came out with a white flag to surrender the town. A Pennsylvania trooper wrote, "It looked to us ridiculous as just now anything we wanted we took, but these people have been so deluded by their papers that they are under the impression that to burn houses and rob them of all we can carry off is our mission here, and they are relieved when they find the mistake."

As Abraham Lincoln walked the streets of Richmond with his youngest son, Stoneman moved to Christiansburg by midnight of April 4-5. Palmer's Brigade destroyed the railroad track of the Virginia and Tennessee Railroad east of Christiansburg. Brown's Brigade did the same west of the town. The troopers deceived telegraph operators in Lynchburg and had the Black women of Christiansburg cooking for them. Other regiments took possession of the railroad bridges and ferries over the New River and another detachment destroyed the bridge over the Roanoke River. With four separate detachments spread out over one hundred and fifty miles of track, the Virginia and Tennessee Railroad ceased operation.

Stoneman sent 250 of the 15th Pennsylvania Cavalry under Major Wagner to Salem, Virginia. Stoneman sent Major Wagner and 250 men of the 15th Pennsylvania Cavalry to destroy the railroad bridges around Salem, Virginia. They reached Salem on

April 5 via Bent Mountain "over a most wretched road." Once there they destroyed wagons and train cars. On April 7, Wagner reached the Peaks of Otter near the James River. Wagner was across Robert E. Lee's avenue of retreat on the outskirts of Lynchburg the next day. Wagner hesitated to destroy covered bridges over the Big and Little Otter Rivers as he hoped the war would end, but eventually destroyed them. He returned to Stoneman after riding over 300 miles (including 84 miles in 42 hours) and avoiding the troops at Lynchburg and Martinsville. He avoided the latter quietly ordering the men to hold their sabers and no fires.

On the return of Stoneman's main force from Christiansburg to North Carolina, Palmer mistakenly went through Martinsville. General Gillem in his report said, "Colonel Palmer, commanding the First Brigade had been directed to send the Tenth Michigan directly on the railroad to Martinsville, by some misunderstanding he marched with his entire command."

On April 7, 1865, the entire command except for Wagner began to move towards North Carolina. The direct route ran through Patrick County. Robert E. Lee lost 7,000 men along the banks of Sayler's Creek near present day Farmville, Virginia, the day before as Grant's forces under the command of Sheridan closed in on Lee.

Virtually untouched by Union troops on its soil during the Civil War, Patrick County, Virginia, saw a change in the spring of 1865. During the second week of April 1865, a lone horse carried Dr. William F. B. Taylor of Elamsville, Virginia, on his daily rounds. Suddenly, in the distance, horse and rider glimpsed some of the 4,500 cavalry under the command of George Stoneman. Dr. Taylor and friend prudently jumped a fence and raced into the forest. The animal spent the evening tied to a tree and the doctor spent the night at a friend's home.

Gillem's report states: "At 2 p.m. the march was resumed and at 10 p.m. we arrived at Taylorsville, Virginia. Remained at Taylorsville during the 8th."

The Second and Third brigades came through Patrick County and stopped on the evening of April 7. Theodore Mallaby, a Second Lieutenant in the newly formed Signal Corps wrote in a report in the *Official Records of the War of the Rebellion*, "April 6th command moved at 7 p.m. to Taylorsville via Jacksonville crossing the Blue Ridge at Mowbrey Gap. Went into camp at Taylorsville at 11 pm after marching a distance of 48 miles. April 9 marched at 7 am to Danbury." General Stoneman stayed in Taylorsville, now Stuart, until the morning of the ninth with the majority of his command.

Stoneman's raiders received blame for many incidents in Patrick County at the end of the war. Problems with the jail are nothing new in the history of the "Free State." The condition of the jail plagued county officials throughout the Civil War. Early in the war, Floyd County held prisoners for Patrick County and Henry County did the same in 1863. The war produced larger numbers of prisoners and the facility in Patrick could not safely hold them. In 1862, the county charged the Confederate government $10.30 and Virginia $23.40 for jailing deserters. In October 1862, the "Gentleman Justices" voted to build a new jail and appointed a committee to look into a new jail for the county. Commissioners Crawford Turner and Silas Carter advertised to build a jail in July 1864, but received no bid within the limits. In October 1865, the Order Book stated the county could no longer use the jail.

In May 1896, Supervisor's Order Book #2 reports that the

"repairing or building of a new jail be deferred until the board can ascertain something definite in regard to the claim of the county which is now pending in Congress against the U. S. for the jail that was burned at the close of the war." The county paid Mr. C. A. Powell for taking depositions relating to the burning of the jail. Claude Swanson, representing the Fifth District including Patrick County in the United States House of Representatives of the Fifty-Fourth Congress, petitioned the War Claims Committee on April 30 to look into the possibility of funds to build a jail. The claim presented in the bill H. R. 8606 stated that the jail burned at the end of the war and the county deserved compensation of $10,000 for the damages. There is no official record of this claim's acceptance or funds allocated. The bill never reached the House floor for a vote and apparently died in committee. Stoneman's raid burned the jail in Boone, North Carolina, during the raid that included his visit to Patrick County, but that action took place in answer to an attack by local forces.

The timing of this action, taken in context, leads to an alternative reasoning. Grover Cleveland, the only Democrat elected President of the United States between James Buchannan and Woodrow Wilson was in his last term. Cleveland, sympathetic to the South, in a very controversial move returned Confederate Battle Flags to several states. Acting in this climate county officials and Swanson may have hoped to receive some patronage before the Republicans took back the White House. On August 15, 1896, the Supervisors authorized the building of a home for the jailer and a few months later authorized the repair of the roof of the courthouse and jail along with new cells of "Bessemer steel" without funding from the United States of America.

The Southern Claims Commission in the National Archives contain several claims from citizens. Thomas Shelton claimed that Stoneman's men took one mare, 300 pounds of bacon, twenty-five bushels of corn, one rifle, 500 pounds of fodder, twenty-five fowls and two silver watches. Shelton's claim was one of two accepted by the commission in 1878.

On April 9, a Union trooper reported, "Started at 2 in the morning, passing through a fine section of the country, the home of the aristocratic Virginia tobacco planters. The houses are beautiful. Tobacco is so plentiful that all are smoking very fair cigars. We captured some fine horses, for although all the stock has been run off in the woods, the Negroes tell us where they are concealed, and if have time we go and get them." This same day Stoneman's entire command reunited in Danbury, North Carolina.

Another incident involved fifteen-year-old Richard Joshua Reynolds. The future tobacco magnate hid the family's horses in the woods during the raid. He returned to the family home, Rock Spring, to find it pillaged, but not burned. The raiders only took what they needed to feed themselves and their animals. A man named Staples gave a box of valuables to a poor man living in an obscure place. A malicious neighbor led some of the raiders to the poor man's house and took the treasure. Later, Staples traveled to Danbury to ask for his possessions back and received them.

Gillem's report states: "The number of Negroes who were following the column had increased to such an extent as to endanger the safety of the command in case it should become closely engaged with the enemy. Several hundred were sent from this point (April 10) to East Tennessee under a sufficient guard for their protection. They all reached their destination in safety and most of those fit for military service I have since learned are in Colonel Bartlett's 119th USCT."

Many slaves followed George Stoneman's United States cavalry when it passed through in April 1865. The Reynolds' slaves followed the Yankee raiders. Hardin Reynolds told his other son Abram, "My son the Yankees have been here and torn up everything and my Negro men have all gone with them." Upon arriving in Danbury, Stoneman felt the number of former slaves following the raid endangered the future safety of all involved. Stoneman sent "several hundred" under guard to East Tennessee, where many of the men enlisted in the 119th United States Colored Troops. The regiment organized at Camp Nelson near Nicholasville, Kentucky, from January 18 until May 16, 1865. Equipped with .577 caliber Enfield rifles, George Gray, Peter Gray, Edmond Hylton, Jacob Reynolds, Miles Reynolds and Samuel Tatum of Patrick County served under Colonel Charles G. Bartlett and Lieutenant Colonel Thomas R. Weaver. The regiment mustered out of the service of the United States on April 27, 1866.

Dr. Gary W. Gallagher at the University of Virginia say that the Civil War "still speaks to our condition today." Arguments over the size of government involving states' rights still resonate today. Just look at the controversies over gay marriage and whether states or the national government should decide such questions. We need only look at the problem of race in our country. Whether it is integration or reparations to understand each other, black and white, we need to also understand what the slaves of African descent went through and the effect it has on their descendants today.

Jefferson Davis, President of the Confederacy, a day's ride away in Danville wrote Jubal Early's brother, Samuel, that day asking him to report to Robert E. Lee "information as to movements of the enemy through Patrick." Unknown to Davis and Stoneman on April 9, 1865, Robert E. Lee met Ulysses S. Grant to surrender the Army of Northern Virginia to the Army of the Potomac at Appomattox Court House, Virginia.

Stoneman's raid continued down into Piedmont North Carolina going through Germanton and Bethania on the way to Salisbury. They described Germanton as, "without paint or whitewash, and laziness is apparent all over it."

Stoneman sent Palmer throughout the countryside. On April 10, the mayors of Winston and Salem came out to surrender their towns. The Moravians and Quakers of Piedmont North

Carolina, who favored peace and the Union, were happy to see them. A soldier wrote, "Here we met with a most cordial reception, very different from the usual greetings we receive. The ladies cheered us, and brought out bread, pies and cakes...The people showed much enthusiasm at the sight of the flag we carried, and many were the touching remarks made about it."

Other opinions were present in Salem. A young woman at Salem Female Academy from Alabama waved a Confederate flag and shouted a rebel yell. The town clerk reported to one of the Yankee troopers, "You can't get our horses; We got'em hid in the cellar." A local newspaper reported, "The Federals strictly respected private persons and property."

Palmer sent Betts with the 15th Pennsylvania Cavalry to destroy railroad bridges between Greensboro and Danville. That same day, April 10, Jefferson Davis left Danville for Greensboro. He narrowly missed capture at the Dan River Bridge on the Piedmont Railroad.

Members of the 10th Michigan Cavalry went after railroad bridges between Greensboro and Salisbury including groups going to High Point, Lexington and Thomasville. Stoneman reached the

Shallow Ford on the Yadkin on April 11. Palmer left Salem to rejoin the command.

For several reasons the next target of General Stoneman was Salisbury, North Carolina. A munitions factory there producing arms and ammunitions for the Confederacy employed 240 men and 60 women. The town contained a commissary headquarters and a large hospital in fifteen buildings and the town's churches. Lastly, the town's prison camp contained over 10,000 Union soldiers. A young woman of the town reported on April 3, "People are looking for Stoneman to come here, his object seems to be to burn bridges. I have heard that the Yankees were only thirteen miles from Mr. Hairston's yesterday." Stoneman's men did not destroy Peter Hairston's house, Cooleemee, in Davie County.

Ulysses S. Grant, commanding all United States Armies, suspended prisoner exchanges in September 1864 resulting in the large number of prisoners in Salisbury. Confederate officials failed to get Grant to resume prisoner exchanges. He wished to apply the extra pressure of caring for Union soldiers on the Southern war effort. The prison is notable for several things. Prisoners played the first baseball game played in North Carolina. Many of the Yankee soldiers "galvanized," joining the Confederate service to escape being a prisoner. At one point in the war, there were 1,427 prisoners, 251 were sick, and one died. For the first quarter of 1862, there were 509 sick and only 3 died. These numbers made the prison a model of humanity compared with others on both sides. In February 1865, due to William T. Sherman's presence in North Carolina and Joseph E. Johnston replacing P. G. T. Beauregard in command of the Confederates, officials evacuated the prisoners from Salisbury except for the sick and lame.

Stoneman's men burned the prison, foundry, arsenal and other buildings on April 12. Some of the destruction included: 1 million rounds of ammo, 10,000 artillery rounds, 6,000 pounds of powder, 10,000 bushels of corn, 75,000 uniforms, 250,000 blankets, 6,000 pounds of bacon, 100,000 pounds of salt, 20,000 pounds of sugar and 15 million dollars in Confederate money.

Palmer wrote, "We burned down the infamous Salisbury prison as we came along that way. It is only necessary to see one of these prison lots to know that the suffering inflicted has been intentional. Why leave thousands of men without a plank to shelter them from the sun or storm, compelling them to burrow in the ground and live like muskrats, when there is a primeval forest adjoining Salisbury, from which a small daily detail of these prisoners could fit us substantial shelter in a week? You can see murder on the face of it."

Van Noppen wrote, "Stoneman's moderation in the treatment of civilians evoked surprise and respect from southerners who had expected worse treatment, basing their fears on depredations of bushwhackers who called themselves soldiers and on newspaper accounts of Sherman's march through Georgia." Twenty-four year old Margaret Beall wrote of the attack on Salisbury by Stoneman's forces: "The missiles were flying thick and fast around and upon the house. Then plunging their horses over the fence, some of the soldiers rushed into the hall and up the steps demanding of me 'the damned rebel who lives here' Downstairs the men were ransacking, pillaging, wielding their swords among the terrified servants and shouting 'Make me some coffee! Fry me some meat! Make me some bread or I'll cut you in two!" Another resident of the town stated that, "Salisbury's people will always hold Stoneman in grateful remembrance for the strict control he exercised over his troops."

On April 12, the Army of Northern Virginia of nearly 30,000 men representing about 25% of Confederate forces surrendered at Appomattox Court House, Virginia.

Stoneman's only failure of the raid occurred six miles north of Salisbury at the North Carolina Railroad bridge over the Yadkin River when 1,000 men under Brigadier General Zebulon York fought off Miller. Included in the Confederate forces were 200 "galvanized" Yankees from the prison and one former northerner, John C. Pemberton, who in July 1863 commanded the Confederates at Vicksburg, Mississippi, and who now staffed an artillery piece for York.

The next day, April 13, Statesville hosted the Yankee raiders continuing the trend already exhibited by Tarheel males. A woman of town remarked, "Their return with the news that they brought, was a signal for a general movement of the male population toward the friendly forests." Mrs. Zebulon Vance, wife of North Carolina's Governor, witnessed Union troopers dividing the contents of her trunk. Stoneman returned the contents with his apologies. On April 14, Stoneman at Taylorsville, North Carolina, heard of Lee's surrender. Palmer spent April 14-17 in Statesville. Government stores, the railroad depot and the Iredell Express newspaper, "a paper which was obnoxious from the war with which it had advocated the cause of the Confederacy" were destroyed.

That night, Mary and Abraham Lincoln attended a play "Our American Cousin" at Ford's Theater in Washington, D. C. Earlier that day Lincoln, speaking of Jefferson Davis and the Confederate government said, "Let them go. We don't want to be bothered with them. Frighten them out of the country." Around 10 p.m. actor John Wilkes Booth shot President Lincoln in the back of the head and did more harm than any other Confederate bullet. Plots to kill Vice-President Andrew Johnson and Secretary of State Henry Seward failed.

Abraham Lincoln died early the next morning, April 15, 1865, causing rage in the North and a mixed reaction in the South. William T. Sherman said, "Of all the men I ever met he seemed to possess more of the elements of greatness, combined with goodness, than any other." The fleeing President of the Confederate States of America reportedly said, "We have lost our best friend in the court of the enemy." Jefferson Davis told an aide, "I certainly have no special regard for Mr. Lincoln but there are great many men of whose end I would rather hear than his." One of those Davis would rather see die was Governor Vance of North Carolina, who wrote of Davis after meeting him in Charlotte that he was "absolutely blind...to those things which his prejudice or hope did not desire to see."

The next morning, April 16, from Lenoir "a rebellious little hole," Stoneman returned to Tennessee via Watauga County, his raid complete, with prisoners bound for Camp Chase, Ohio. The purpose of the raid had been to bring the war to the people of a region virtually untouched. It did a good job of destroying railroad bridges and tearing up track in Lee's line of retreat, but failed to free the Union prisoners at Salisbury. The officers behaved as gentlemen and restrained their soldiers, frequently protecting homes. Stoneman's time in Patrick County was a rest halt for his men before they moved back into North Carolina. The raiders' diversion into Southwest Virginia caused the people of North Carolina to ease up, and when the raiders returned, they caught the populace off guard. Historians described this raid as "splendidly conceived, an ably executed attack upon the war potential and the civilian population of the south." A more civilized example of "Total War" than other more famous Union excursions into the South brought home to our area the power of Union forces.

Stoneman divided his forces with Gillem moving towards Asheville before he returned to Tennessee. Ina W. Van Noppen comments on this move, "Now that Stoneman had left the command the plundering and sacking of houses and mutilation of furnishings greatly increased." Palmer watched the Catawba River at Lincolnton, where the locals commented that his men "protected" them "from violence or molestation."

Gillem moved towards Asheville via Morganton, Rutherford, where he sacked the town after taking its surrender, leaving for Tennessee and returned on April 26. "Asheville will never again hear such sounds and witness such scenes—pillage of every character, and destruction the most wanton."

Even Union soldiers were disgusted with Miller and the "homegrown Yankees." One of Palmer's men wrote, "These Tennesseans in their present condition do not add any strength to the Union forces. In the beginning and during most of the war they had suffered terrible cruelties at the hands of the rebels. They had been hunted and shot down as unworthy of any humanity being shown them. Their homes were burned and their families driven away, and all because they were loyal to the flag, but now that the tables were turned and disloyal families were at their mercy, they repaid what they had suffered by an indiscriminate pillage. The result was a demoralized command, out of which little military duty could be had; and their General knew they were in no condition to fight an organized force, no matter how small."

On April 18, Joseph E. Johnston met with William T. Sherman at the Bennett Place near Durham Station to surrender his army. Sherman offered such lenient terms that the new President Andrew Johnson, a pro-Union Tennessean, rejected the terms. Sherman offered to take the surrender of all Confederate forces, recognize the present state governments as legitimate, respect the political rights of former Confederates and issue a general amnesty. On April 26, Union troops killed John Wilkes Booth in a barn in Virginia. Johnston and Sherman met again to surrender the former's army of around 35,000 men.

Twenty-six years later, 82 year old Joseph E. Johnston stood bare headed in the rain as an honorary pallbearer at the funeral of Sherman. When asked if he should cover himself Johnston replied, "If I were in his place, and he was standing here in mine, he would not put on his hat." Johnston caught a cold and died ten days after showing respect to his former adversary.

Palmer stayed in western North Carolina until receiving a message from George Thomas on April 23 to "pursue Jefferson Davis to the ends of the earth, if necessary, and never give up." Union officials offered $100,000 in gold for his capture. Palmer moved into South Carolina and then Georgia crossing the Savannah River north of Augusta. Palmer acted as a flanking agent on Davis' retreat. He captured Confederate Generals Bragg and Wheeler.

Davis spent April 20-26 in Charlotte, North Carolina, crossed into South Carolina and by May 4 was in Georgia. On May 10, Union cavalry captured President Davis near Irwinville, Georgia. One participant said that Union General Wilson held the bag and Palmer drove the game into it. Two days later, the Confederates won the last battle of the war near Brownsville,

Texas.

Alvan C. Gillem became colonel of the 28th Infantry in 1866 and commander of the Fourth Military District including Mississippi and Arkansas. He fell out of favor with Radical Republicans for his "conciliatory and moderate" views towards the former Confederates after Grant replaced Andrew Johnson as President. Gillem died at his home, Soldier's Rest, near Nashville in 1875.

After the war, Stoneman commanded the Department of Tennessee headquarter in Memphis. He opposed the policies of the "Radical Republicans" during Reconstruction. Stoneman commanded the First Military District, Virginia from June 1868 until April 1869 and the Department of Arizona until his retirement in May 1871. He bought a 400 acre estate near in the San Gabriel Valley near San Marino, California, called "The Oaks." President Rutherford B. Hayes appointed him to the Board of Indian Commissioners. He served as Commissioner of Transportation and became a Democratic Governor of California from 1883 until 1887. In July 1885, fire destroyed his home along with his papers and mementos from the Civil War. He became estranged from his wife over an alleged affair she denied having. George Stoneman returned to New York in poor health and broken financially. In 1894, he had surgery for his recurring hemorrhoid problem and died in Jamestown on September 5, 1894, while visiting a sister. He rests today in Bentley Cemetery in Lakewood, New York.

To paraphrase Aunt Pittypat of *Gone With The Wind*, "Yankees in Mount Airy, How did they ever get in?" The answer Major General George Stoneman, shown above, led a cavalry raid in the closing days of the Civil War that came through Mount Airy April 2-3, 1865. The day that Robert E. Lee evacuated Richmond, over 4,000 blue-coated troopers camped on the Ararat River along the Hamburg Street. These men left from near Knoxville, Tennessee, on March 21 and came across the Appalachian Mountains to Boone and along the Yadkin River to Rockford before turning north through Surry County to Mount Airy. They left after raiding the post office and chased after a wagon train towards Hillsville, Virginia, before making their way all the way to Christiansburg and the Virginia and Tennessee Railroad before returning to North Carolina. (Courtesy of the Library of Congress.)

Andy Griffith with his parents, Carl and Geneva Nunn Griffith.

Afterword

Andy's Civil War

Following "Stonewall" Jackson was tough on many men during the War Between the States. The only way to avoid service was death, sickness, or a wound. Andrew J. Nunn of North Carolina found himself as part of the latter as his compatriots in the 21st North Carolina Infantry Regiment moved down to the peninsula between the James and York Rivers to fight with Robert E. Lee's Army of Northern Virginia in the summer of 1862.

Nunn found himself left behind at Mount Jackson, Virginia, in the Shenandoah Valley at the beginning of June 1862. Although Mount Jackson was not named for Thomas J. Jackson, who received his famous sobriquet "Stonewall" at the Battle of First Manassas as the Southerners called it, the valley became famous for the exploits of Jackson, the former VMI Professor. The Yankees called it First Bull Run when South Carolinian General Bee told his men to "look at Jackson standing like a stonewall."

Nunn probably received a wound at the First Battle of Winchester on May 25, 1861. The regiment lost 21 killed and 60 wounded. Serving under Richard Ewell's Division in the brigade of Isaac Trimble, Nunn saw some hot action. One internet blogger described it this way. "Dawn of May 25th found Banks' forces defensively positioned on a range of protective hills just south of the town. Jackson launched assaults on both Federal flanks and immediately encountered fierce resistance. On the Confederate right, near the Front Royal road, Trimble ordered his "two Twenty Firsts" to charge a strongly positioned Union regiment. A member of the 21st North Carolina described the ensuing charge: "With a wild cheer the regiment moved swiftly towards the enemy's line behind stone walls, and was met by a most terrific fire of infantry and grape shot. The regiment moved right on to the stone wall, from which the enemy were pouring forth a perfect storm of canister and minie balls from right and left–cross-firing upon us." Despite initially wavering in the intense fire, the Carolinians regrouped and joined their brothers in the 21st Georgia in driving the Federals from the field."

Nunn possibly was one of thirteen wounded at Cross Keys and Port Republic culminating Jackson's Valley Campaign, one of the most famous military maneuvers in history. Andy Nunn recovered from his wound to fight on.

He had brothers in the war. Private Jefferson Nunn died at age 24 on September 25, 1861, at Thoroughfare Gap near Manassas, Virginia, of "typhoid fever." Another brother, Private William H. Nunn enlisted with his two brothers on June 13, 1861, and was present until October 1864.

The Nunns were part of the "Mountain Boys" that enlisted on May 29, 1861, in Danbury, Stokes County, North Carolina. The men traveled to nearby Danville, Virginia, where they became Company F of the 21st North Carolina Infantry Regiment (11th North Carolina Volunteers). The regiment included men from Davidson, Surry, Forsyth, Stokes, Rockingham, and Guilford counties.

Andrew Nunn enlisted as a Private at age 26. Other than reported sick in October 1861, his early time in the war was not memorable. Eleven months later, his compatriots elected him 3rd Lieutenant on April 26, 1862. By June 1, he was in the hospital at Mount Jackson. He returned to duty and received promotion to 2nd Lieutenant on August 28.

The area around Winchester was not lucky for Andrew Nunn. Two years later as part of the 2nd Corps of the Army of

Northern Virginia under General Jubal Early in Lewis's Brigade on July 20, 1864, he received a wound in the left thigh that broke his femur. Family tradition holds that he lost his leg. His luck ran out at Stephenson's Depot, when Union forces captured him. He spent the rest of the war in either Federal Hospitals or Prisoner of War Camps.

On May 9, 1865, Nunn was at Fort McHenry, Maryland, where Frances Scott Key received his inspiration to write the Star Spangled Banner five decades earlier. Union General Lewis Wallace, who later wrote *Ben Hur,* signed the order transferring Nunn from the General Hospital in Baltimore. On June 24, Nunn took the Oath of Allegiance and was released ending Andy Nunn's Civil War.

Few references to the Civil War are mentioned on The Andy Griffith Show except for one memorable episode "The Loaded Goat" from 1963. Sheriff Andy Taylor tells a lady, who called the Sherriff's office, that the blasting she is hearing out on the highway is not the Yankees attacking Mayberry and he assures her that the South is still holding on to Richmond, Virginia, the Capital of the Confederates States of America.

Years later, the daughter of his younger brother Samuel named her only son after the two Nunn brothers. Geneva Nunn called him Andy Samuel Griffith. He went on to be the most famous person to come from Mount Airy, Surry County, North Carolina.

Confederate Veteran Statue at the University of North Carolina at Chapel Hill known as "Silent Sam"

Bibliography

Manuscripts

Southern Historical Collection, Wilson Library, University of North Carolina-Chapel Hill.
April 17, 1858, Victoria Stuart to Bettie Hairston
September 29, 1855, J. E. B. Stuart to Bettie Hairston
January 4, 1855, J. E. B. Stuart to Bettie Hairston
Christopher Wrenn Bunker Letters.

Surry County Historical Society
Ruth Minnick Papers

Newspapers
Mount Airy News November 11, 1897
Mount Airy Times May 21, 1971
Mount Airy News July 27, 1997
Mount Airy News August 3, 1997
Yadkin Valley News June 9, 1892

Books and Articles
Bryant, Jessie Bunker. *The Connected Bunkers*. Winston-Salem, NC, 2001.
Carter, Carrie Y. and William F. Jr. *Footprints in the Hollows*. Elkin, NC., 1976.
Curtis, George T. *The Life of James Buchanan*. New York, 1883.
Fries, Adelaide. *Forsyth: A County on the March,* UNC 1949.
Gerard, Philip. *Indivisible: Eng and Chang Bunker*. Our State Magazine Volume 2, Number 2, November 2012.
Hairston, Peter. W. *J. E. B. Stuart's Letters To His Hairston Kin, 1850-1855*. North Carolina Historical Review Volume LI, July 1974, No. 3 pp 261-332.
Hartley, Chris J. *Stoneman's 1865 Raid*. Winston-Salem NC, 2010.
Hartley, Chris J. *Stuart's Tarheels.* Gaithersburg, MD. 1996.
Harrell, Roger H. *The 2nd North Carolina Cavalry.* 2011.

Hollingsworth, J. G. *History of Surry County*. 1937.

Jackson, Hester Bartlett. *Surry County Soldiers in the Civil War*. Charlotte, NC. 1992.

Moore, James B. *The Works of James Buchanan*. Volume 12

Powell, William S. What's in a Name?: Why We're All Called Tar Heels http://alumni.unc.edu/article.aspx?sid=3516

Raiford, Neil Hunter. *4th North Carolina Cavalry in the Civil War: A History and Roster*. North Wilkesboro, NC, 2006.

Rosenberg, R. B. Editor. *"For the Sake of My Country" The Diary of Colonel W. W. Ward 9th Tennessee Cavalry, Morgan's Brigade CSA*. Murfreesboro, TN, 1992.

Scott, J. L. *36th and 37th Battalions Virginia Cavalry*. Lynchburg VA, 1986.

Taylor, Michael W. *Tar Heels: How North Carolinians Got Their Nickname*. Raleigh, NC, 1999.

Twain, Mark. *The Siamese Twins*. http://twain.lib.virginia.edu/wilson/siamese.html

Twain, Mark. *Pudd'nhead Wilson and Those Extraordinary Twins*. New York, 2005.

Walker, Marjorie T. *The Gallaways of Rose Hill*. Journal of Rockingham County History and Genealogy Volume IV, June 1979, No. 1

Wallace, Amy and Irving. *The Two*. New York, 1978.

Wolfe, Thomas. *You Can't Go Home Again*. New York, 1942.

Index

A

Appomattox, 188, 193
Ararat River, 201
Ararat, Virginia, 156, 176, 215
Army of Northern Virginia, 158, 171, 175, 188, 193
Augusta, Georgia, 155, 198

B

Bartlett, 187, 188
Beauregard, 171, 191
Bentley, 165, 200
Betts, 165, 189
Blakemore, 78
Boothe, 194, 198
Brown, 71, 73, 165, 180, 215
Buchannan, 185

C

Carter, 166, 183
Chancellorsville, 161
Chickamauga, 163
Civil War, 2
Cleveland, 184
Confederate States of America, 68
Couch, 160
Crawford, 183
Custer, 69, 71, 74, 169

D

Dan River, 190
Davis, 158, 160, 188, 190, 194, 195, 198

E

Early, 183, 188
Echols, 175
Elkin, North Carolina, 171

F

Floyd, 179, 183
Fredericksburg, 161
Fry, 193

G

Gallagher, 186
Geneva Nunn Griffith, 4
Gettysburg, 155
Gillem, 70, 71, 164, 169, 170, 179, 181, 182, 187, 196, 199
Gordon, 170
Grant, U. S., 158, 171, 188, 190
Gray, 188
Griffith, 72, 176
Gwyn, 172

H

Hairston, 190
Hamburg Street, 201
Hardin, 187
Hardisty, 161
Harrison, 165
Henry County, 2
Hill., 215
Hillsville, 201
Hobbs, 155
Hooker, 161
Hylton, 188

J

J. E. B. Stuart, 2
Jackson, 68, 69, 160
Jefferson, 158, 160, 188, 190, 194, 195, 198
Johnson, 164, 168, 194, 197, 199
Johnston, 158, 160, 167, 191, 197, 198

K

Keogh, 71, 169

L

Laurel Hill (Birthplace of J. E. B. Stuart), 215
Lee, 74, 158, 163, 164, 171, 175, 182, 194, 195, 201
Lee, Robert E., 158, 160, 171, 175, 181, 182, 188
Leonard, 67
Lester, 2
Lincoln, 158, 168, 180, 194
Little Bighorn, 71

M

Main Street, 68
Mallaby, 166, 178, 182
Martinsville, 2
Martinsville, Virginia, 181
McClellan, 159, 161
Miller, 70, 165, 178, 179, 193, 197
Minick, 72
Minnick, 156
Moore, 67
Mount Airy, North Carolina, 2, 156, 176

N

Nelson, 188

P

Palmer, 69, 165, 169, 170, 171, 172, 180, 181, 189, 190, 192, 194, 196, 197, 198, 199
Patrick County, 2, 163, 172, 182, 183, 184, 185, 186, 187, 188, 196, 215
Patterson, 169
Pemberton, 193
Perry, 157, 215, 216
Petersburg, 158, 163, 171, 175
Pickett, 155, 160
Powell, 184
Prescott, 155

R

Renfro, 67
Reno, 160

Reynolds, 186, 187
Richmond, 157, 158, 159, 161, 163, 165, 175, 180
Robertson, 157, 186, 215
Rockford Street, 72

S

Schofield, 162
Seward, 194
Shelton, 185
Sheridan, 171, 182
Sherman, 155, 158, 159, 161, 163, 166, 167, 191, 192, 195, 197, 198
Siamese Twins, 78
Smith, 165
Staples, 186
Stoneman, 69, 70, 71, 155, 156, 157, 159, 160, 161, 162, 163, 166, 167, 168, 169, 170, 171, 175, 178, 180, 181, 182, 183, 184, 185, 186, 187, 188, 189, 190, 191, 192, 193, 194, 195, 196, 199, 201
Stuart, 73, 74, 161, 163, 170, 179, 183, 215
Stuart, James Ewell Brown "jeb", 163
Stuart, James Ewell Brown "Jeb", 215
Sturgis, 160
Surry County, 67, 68, 69, 78, 201
Surry County Historical Society, 67, 68, 78
Surry County, North Carolina, 171, 172
Swanson, 184, 185

T

Tatum, 188
Taylor, 182
Taylorsville, 179, 182, 183, 194
Texas, 160, 199
Thomas, George H., 163
Tillson, 169
Trowbridge, 165
Tullahoma, 165
Turner, 183

U

University of Virginia, 186

V

Van Noppen, 156, 192, 196
Vance, 194, 195
Virginia Tech, 186, 215

W

Wagner, 181
War Between the States, 68, 78

Weaver, 188
Wheeler, 198
Wilcox, 160
Wilson, 185, 199
Wytheville, Virginia, 178

Y

Yadkin River, 201
York, 159, 164, 193, 200

Author Tom Perry at J. E. B. Stuart's Birthplace.

About Thomas D. Perry

J. E. B. Stuart's biographer Emory Thomas describes Tom Perry as "a fine and generous gentleman who grew up near Laurel Hill, where Stuart grew up, has founded J. E. B. Stuart Birthplace, and attracted considerable interest in the preservation of Laurel Hill. He has started a symposium series about aspects of Stuart's life to sustain interest in Stuart beyond Ararat, Virginia." Perry holds a BA in History from Virginia Tech in 1983.

Perry started the J. E. B. Stuart Birthplace Preservation Trust, Inc. in 1990. The non-profit organization preserved 75 acres of the Stuart property including the house site where James Ewell Brown Stuart was born on February 6, 1833. Perry wrote the original eight interpretive signs about Laurel Hill's history along with the Virginia Civil War Trails sign and the new Virginia Historical Highway Marker in 2002. He spent many years researching traveling all over the nation to find Stuart materials including two trips across the Mississippi River to visit nearly every place "Jeb" Stuart served in the United States Army (1854-1861). Tom can be seen on Virginia Public Television's *Forgotten Battlefields: The Civil War in Southwest Virginia* with his mentor noted Civil War Historian, Dr. James I. Robertson, Jr. Perry has begun a collection of papers relating to Stuart and Patrick County history in the Special Collections Department of the Carol M. Newman Library at Virginia Tech under the auspices of the Virginia Center For Civil War Studies.

In 2004, Perry began the Free State Of Patrick Internet History Group, which has become the largest historical organization in the area with over 500 members. It covers Patrick County Virginia and regional history. Tom produces a monthly email newsletter about regional history entitled Notes From The Free State of Patrick that goes from his website www.freestateofpatrick.com.

Historian Thomas D. Perry is the author and publisher of over twenty books on regional history in Virginia surrounding his home county of Patrick. In 2009, Perry used his book Images of America Henry County Virginia to raise over $25,000 for the Bassett Historical Center, "The Best Little Library in Virginia," and as editor of the Henry County Heritage Book raised another $30,000. Perry was responsible for over $200,000 of the $800,000 raised to expand the regional history library.

He is the recipient of the John E. Divine Award from the Civil War Education Association, the Hester Jackson Award from the Surry County Civil War Round Table, and the Best Article Award from the Society of North Carolina Historians for his article on Stoneman's Raid in 2008.

Perry also recently received the National Society of the Daughters of the American Revolution Community Service Award from the Patrick Henry Chapter Daughters of the American Revolution.

In 2010, he received acknowledgement from the Bassett Public Library Association for his work to expand the Bassett Historical Center. Perry was named Henry County Virginia Man of the Year by www.myhenrycounty.com.

Perry recently was seen on Henrico County Virginia's documentary *Bold Cavalier* about the life of J. E. B. Stuart. He speaks all over the nation of Stuart and the Civil War and still lives outside his birthplace Mount Airy, North Carolina, in Patrick County, Virginia.

Made in the USA
Middletown, DE
25 May 2023

30720079R00126